Controversies in Sociology
edited by
Professor T. B. Bottomore and Dr M. J. Mulkay

3

Socialism
The Active Utopia

Socialism
The Active Utopia

by

ZYGMUNT BAUMAN
Professor of Sociology, University of Leeds

London
George Allen & Unwin Ltd
Ruskin House   Museum Street

First published in 1976

ISBN 0 04 300059 2 *hardback*
0 04 300060 5 *paperback*

Printed in Great Britain
in 10 point Times Roman type
by Clarke, Doble & Brendon Ltd.
Plymouth

To Irena and Lydia —
my twin utopias

'No man can put forth any special claim in the face of Nature; but in society want at once becomes an injustice either to this class or to that.'

HEGEL

Contents

1

Utopia and Reality

Socialism descended upon nineteenth-century Europe as utopia.

This statement is bound to provoke one of two responses: either of angry protests from those who feel safer on a sturdy jeep of historical necessity than on a flying carpet of human will; or of friendly smiles from those who feel that the world we live in would be a much happier place were it never haunted by the abortive venture into equality. Both protests and smiles are – I admit – more than partly justified by the sense in which the concept of 'utopia' has sedimented in the public mind. But it is not the sense in which I propose to use it.

The context in which the word 'utopia' appears most often in everyday discourse is the phrase condemning an idea, a project, an expectation as a 'mere utopia'. The phrase marks the end, not the beginning of an argument; one can still quarrel, to be sure, whether the verdict applies to a particular case, but provided it does, further consideration of the possible merits of the idea in question will make little sense. The indictment amounts to a flip and irrevocable dismissal of the idea as a figment of unrestrained fantasy, unscientific, at odds with reality – i.e. loaded with all those features which mark off an idea as something to be kept at a safe distance from scholarly discourse.

The operation has been performed often enough to turn it into a purely perfunctory procedure, which no longer requires reference to the original justification. One can only suppose that the disrepute into which utopian thinking has fallen is that shared by magic, religion, and alchemy – all those slushy paths of the errant human mind which modern science set about eliminating once and for all from the map of human action. Having been defined from the outset as an idle, unrealistic blueprint without much basis in reality,

A*

utopia was irretrievably cast among the false ideas which in fact hinder human progress by diverting human effort from the ways of reason and rationality. Stripping Thomas More's term of its intended ambiguity and reducing it to only one of the two originally intertwined meanings – to 'a place which does not exist' (no longer associated with 'a place to be desired', eutopia) – the dominant usage rendered the historical irrelevance of utopia self-verifying. With the benefit of hindsight the blueprints which had materialised were classified as predictions, while the name 'utopia' was kept only for those which failed to do so.

The insufficiency of treating utopias as predictions which turned out to be false, or plans which failed to prove their realism, will become evident if we only agree that each moment of human history is, to a greater or a lesser degree, an open-ended situation; a situation which is not entirely determined by the structure of its own past, and from which more than one string of events may follow (not only in a subjective sense, considering the state of our knowledge, but in the objective sense as well, considering a complete knowledge of the present and the past which could have been collected and processed only if the perfect research and data-processing technology had been available). People, said C. Wright Mills, 'may become aware of predictions made about their activities, and accordingly they can and often do re-direct themselves; they may falsify or fulfil the predictions. Which they will do is not, as yet, subject to very good prediction. In so far as men have some degree of freedom, what they may do will not be readily predictable.'[1] The point which Mills made (a very radical point in a period dominated by the reified, 'reacting' image of man and the behaviouristic paradigm) was that far from being just predictions, passively waiting on bookshelves to be compared with the actual course of events they avowedly tried to foresee, our statements about the future become, from the start, active factors in shaping this future. Which way they will deflect the course of history does not depend on their content alone; it ultimately hinges, one would say, on the intrinsically unpredictable, intractable human praxis. If that is so, then the right question to ask about predictions or, more generally, visions of the future, is not whether they have been verified or falsified by subsequent events, but in which way and to what degree these events have been influenced and generated by the presence of the aforementioned visions in the public mind. Thomas Carlyle called history 'an imprisoned prophecy'; Oscar

Wilde declared that 'a map of the world which does not include Utopia is not worth even glancing at, for it leaves out the one country at which Humanity is always landing'; Anatole France reminded his science-intoxicated contemporaries that 'without the utopians of other times, men would still live in caves, miserable and naked'. And Gabriel Tarde posed the question almost naïve in its pertinence:[2] 'it seems to me neither more nor less conceivable that the future *which is not yet*, should influence the present than that the past, *which is no more*, should do so'. One can see that all these thinkers were trying to grapple not just with the issue of utopia and its active historical role, but with the much wider question of the nature of human history as such.

The radical opposition to the conservative view of culture, as reduced to learning, to the detriment of creativity, starts with an assumption that the peculiarly human mode of existence is founded on a unique phenomenon of the future, as a mode of time qualitatively distinct from the past in the sense of being not-entirely-determined and at the same time sufficiently powerful to destroy, time and again, even the thickest layer of habitual patterns. The most dramatically distinctive feature of culture is the notorious (though hotly denied by many a scientist in the name of the ultimate success of the scientific venture) human ability to decline to learn, to resist the conditioning pressure, to 'make responses' to 'stimuli' which are not present in any imaginable material sense. Inventiveness, originality verging on waywardness, characterise human beings at least as much as their ability to learn and their capacity for being conditioned. Some thinkers would go so far in their protest against the 'learning' image of man that they would take, with Teilhard de Chardin, a stance opposite to the one portrayed above: 'It is finally the Utopians, not the "realists", who make scientific sense. They at least, though their flights of fancy may cause us to smile, have a feeling for the true dimensions of the phenomenon of man'.[3]

Whatever the nature of man as such, the capacity to think in a utopian way does involve the ability to break habitual associations, to emancipate oneself from the apparently overwhelming mental and physical dominance of the routine, the ordinary, the 'normal'. In this respect utopian thinking belongs in the same category as invention, as Raymond Ruyer[4] emphatically pointed out. In our civilisation, built upon the ideal of technical perfection and efficiency, which 'judges men by their fitness for jobs, not jobs by their fitness for men',[5] and in fact accepts the ideal of *technical*, '*Zweck*' perfection as the only ideal admissible in a world bent on instrumentalising ends rather than setting them, invention is an entirely legitimate and, indeed, praiseworthy and prestige-bestowing endeavour; but not utopia, though it involves the same psychological structure and the same propensity for noncompliance and defiance of existing patterns. To quote Ruyer again, a utopian thinker would be just an ordinary sociologist, except for his decision to abandon at some point 'the vehicle of mental experience'[6] in his determined attempt to forestall any deviation from the direction he wishes to pursue. This 'abandoning of the vehicle of experience' is a unifying feature of the inventor and the utopianist; the first, however, pursues technical perfection within the framework delineated by the dominant value-standards, while the utopianist defies the standards themselves, and this makes all the difference in a world bent on *Zweckrationalität*. Virgilio Melchiore places the utopian imagination in the Kantian 'field of mediation' which stretches between the 'consciousness of the absolute' and the 'awareness of the historical situation'.[7] 'The absolute' is one thing for which our civilisation has little use; those who cannot help but suffer from Nietzsche's *Fernstenliebe* are invited to let off steam by diving into the wonderworld of science fiction, famous for its remarkable blend of unbridled technical fantasy and disheartening paucity of imagination in anything concerning human relations. One wonders how far the freedom that people actually enjoy can be measured by the extent to which they are able to envisage worlds different from their own.

These are the reasons why we emphatically reject the scornful view that is manifest in the 'mere utopia' catchphrase. It seems that this phrase reflects more the nature of the social system in which it has become common currency than the value of utopia which it pretends to assess. I think social life cannot in fact be understood unless due attention is paid to the immense role played by utopia. Utopias share with the totality of culture the quality – to paraphrase Santayana – of a knife with the edge pressed against the future. They constantly cause the reaction of the future with the present, and thereby produce the compound known as human history.

I shall now outline the functions which have been played by utopias in general, and by modern socialism in particular, which to my mind substantiate the claim that they have a crucial and con-structive role in the historical process.

1. Utopias relativise the present. One cannot be critical about something that is believed to be an absolute. By exposing the partiality of current reality, by scanning the field of the possible in which the real occupies merely a tiny plot, utopias pave the way for a critical attitude and a critical activity which alone can transform the present predicament of man. The presence of a utopia, the ability to think of alternative solutions to the festering problems of the present, may be seen therefore as a necessary condition of historical change.

Utopias, to be sure, differ from electoral platforms and even from long-term political programmes in that they seem to be little concerned with pragmatically conceived realism. They offer the luxury of unleashing human imagination and leading it to the distant expanses which would never be reached if it were held down by the exactions of the political game. Since the meaning of logic and rationality is defined by the latter rather than the former, 'utopias do not seem logical and immediate steps from what is in existence at present. . . . The utopian vision, in this sense, breaks with historical continuity'.[8] It does not follow, however, that they are useless for the practically-minded reformers of the society. Nor does it follow that nothing but ridicule toward utopias becomes a sober mind bent on 'realistic', i.e. piecemeal, improvement of his society. The situation in which major political blocs of a nation know no better than to argue about the balance of payments and the desirable level of the bank rate signals, in fact, a dangerous drying up of the reservoir of utopian ideas and spells trouble. It is rather the boldness of the utopian insight into the unexplored future, its ability to cut loose and be impractical, which sets the stage for a genuinely realistic politics, one which takes stock of all opportuni-ties contained in the present. The presence of such utopian ideas and their vitality may be seen as a symptom of a society set on a perhaps turbulent, but vigorous development. In Lewis Mumford's words, 'an ideal pattern is the ideological equivalent of a physical container: it keeps extraneous change within the bounds of human purpose. With the aid of ideals, a community may select, among a multitude of possibilities, those which are consonant with its own nature or that promise to further human development. This corresponds to the role of entelechy in Aristotle's biology'.[9] The thin line which divides a genuine realism from downright conservatism disguised as soberness runs between willingness and refusal to consider the full range of human alternatives, however fantastic they may seem from the perspective of a complacent or disenchanted commonsense.

2. Utopias are those aspects of culture (in itself a programme rather than a description of the human condition) in which the possible extrapolations of the present are explored. They seldom raise their eyes very high above the level of current reality; they are, indeed, surprisingly realistic in their drawing from the experience and the cravings of their contemporaries, and in their penchant for singling out this or the other established institution as a vehicle of desired change. No epoch, said Marx, poses problems which it is unable to solve; George Sorel, adding a psychological specification to this historiosophical generalisation, remarked that when a mind puts forth an idea, it is because the idea is in the air. It can hardly be otherwise, since the utopian ideals of any generation – if the generation is lucky and free enough to possess any – are shaped, like culture in general, under the double pressure of the galvanising feeling of deprivation and the chastening squeeze of omnipresent and stubborn realities. On the one hand, Frank E. Mannel says, 'utopia provides what men most keenly miss';[10] on the other, says Fred Charles Iklé, 'we can only follow the light at the prow of our ship'.[11] Both are right, since they focus on two mutually complementary traits of utopian epistemology.

Utopias, so to speak, transcend the level of both theory and practice in their voluntarily modest, immediate sense. They provide answers to issues people experience as poignant; but the question they try to respond to is neither 'what can I know?', which is the concern of philosophers, not 'what ought I do?', which is the domain of ideologues and politicians. It is 'what may I hope?', an awkward question, which Kant would perhaps declare illegitimate, since it invokes simultaneously his 'practical' and 'theoretical' reason, subordinating the second to the first, while remaining stubbornly oblivious to the incompatibility of their structures and potentials. The driving force behind the search for utopia is neither the theoretical nor the practical reason, neither the cognitive nor the moral interest, but the principle of hope; the idea very much present, though somewhat hidden, in Kant's quarrying of the mysteries of reason, but analysed in depth by Ernst Bloch. Hope supplies the missing link between practical and theoretical interests because it is intrinsically critical of the reality in which it is rooted. Again, it extends the meaning of realism to encompass the full range of possible options.

3.   Utopias split the shared reality into a series of competing projects-assessments. The reality in which utopia is rooted is not neutral toward conflicting cognitive perspectives generated by social conflicts. In so far as the society consists of groups differentiated by an unequal share of available goods as well as by unequal access to the means of social action – including the ability to act critically – all criticism of the present is inevitably committed. It may be attributed by the analyst to specific classes or strata whose grievances and cravings it represents, even though the link may be obscured by the largely haphazard social location of the author and his own supra-partisan illusions.

Instead of constituting a class among varieties of human thinking, utopia is an integral element of the critical attitude, which always materialises in a group-specific form, representing a group experience and invariably partisan yearnings. A vision eutopian to one group may well be dystopian to another, not too novel a phenomenon for any student of social and political thought. Utopias, therefore, help to lay bare and make conspicuous the major divisions of interest within a society. They contribute to the crystallisation of major socio-political forces, thereby converting differences of status into differences of action. They scan the options open to society at the current stage of its history; but by exposing their link to the predicament of various groups, utopias reveal also their class-committed nature. In other words, utopias relativise the future into a bundle of class-committed solutions, and dispel the conservative illusion that one and only one thread leads on from the present. If the reality-protecting ideology attempts to disguise history as nature, utopias, on the contrary, unmask the historical status of alleged nature. They portray the future as a set of competing projects, and thereby reveal the role of human volition and concerted effort in shaping and bringing it out. The conservative perspective manifests itself in discussing the future in terms of 'the probable'; the utopian perspective prefers to speak in terms of 'the possible', even if, for the sake of expediency, it chooses to hide behind the mask of 'the inevitable'. The conservative perspective is backed by the ubiquitous power of habit and routine; in order to unleash the self-emancipating effort of those who can expect nothing but a rough deal from an extrapolation of the present, utopias are bound to embark on the hazardous venture of depicting the group-committed ideals, as embodied in the viable and complete social system, with a degree of verisimilitude which can easily be held against them by a scientific purist. But this allegedly unwarranted fantasy is the only tool with which to make up for the handicapped position of an idea which dares to challenge the twin powers of routine behaviour and commonsensical knowledge. The dominant definitions of realism tend to be cut to the measure of dominant interests; they are meant to defend their dominance by defending the habitual and the 'normal'. Utopias weaken the defensive walls of habit, thus preparing their destruction by a dramatic thrust of condensed dissent, or their gradual erosion by the vitriolic solution of utopian ideas.

4.   Utopias do exert enormous influence on the actual course of historical events. Sometimes they are so promptly incorporated into political practice (as was the case with Harrington's *Oceania* and the American Constitution laid down by his admirers) that there is hardly time for the glue to dry under their utopian label; sometimes they are decreed to have been brought into reality and then they imperceptibly merge into conservative ideologies. But in most cases they just linger in the public mind as guides for social action, as criteria marking off the good from the evil, and as obstinate reminders of the never-plugged gap between the promise and the reality, too slow to catch up with its own constitutive ideals. In this triple role utopias enter reality not as the aberrations of deranged intellects, but as powerful factors acting from within what is the only substance of reality, motivated human action. Daniel Bell has traced the logic of much of American history to 'the realisation of the promise of equality which underlies the founding of this country, and the manifestation of the Tocqueville's summation of American democracy: what the few have today, the many will demand tomorrow'.[12] François Bloch-Lainé, invoking semantic distinctions proposed by Gaston Berger, suggests the term 'prospective acting' for the collective action induced by a vision of the goal-system: 'Its starting point is the idea that we can determine a voluntary future, a future that is "never inevitable", provided that we place ourselves resolutely in a future-oriented framework to

influence the present, rather than remain overly impressed by the past.'[13]

This 'activating presence' of utopia in human action is also the only way in which the content of the utopia may be put to a practical test and examined for its degree of 'realism'. There is no method which allows us to establish in advance the 'truth' or 'untruth' of utopia, for the simple reason that the fate of utopia, which hinges in a considerable measure on the occurrence of an appropriately massive social effort, is not determined in advance. Any inventory of supporting and hindering factors is bound to be incomplete without the decisive, yet unpredictable, constituent of an adequate human action. Therefore the 'realism' or 'practicability' of a utopia may be discovered (or, more appropriately, secured) only in the course of action. By summoning such action utopia sets in motion the forces which may bring it to pass; declaring its programme as 'utopian' in the lowly sense we discussed at the outset appears in this light as one of the means by which this 'practical verification' of utopia can be prevented.

To sum up, one can define utopia – in the sense in which it will be used in this study – as an image of a future and better world, which is:

(1) felt as still unfulfilled and requiring an additional effort to be brought about;

(2) perceived as desirable, as a world not so much bound to come as one which should come;

(3) critical of the existing society; in fact a system of ideas remains utopian and thus able to boost human activity only in so far as it is perceived as representing a system essentially different from, if not antithetical to, the existing one;

(4) involving a measure of hazard; for an image of the future to possess the qualities of utopia, it must be ascertained that it will not come to pass unless fostered by a deliberate collective action. Gramsci's well-known view of organised action as the only available way of 'verifying' social predictions fits this attribute of utopia very well.

2

Utopia and the Modern Mind

The four traits above are defining features of utopias as a family of intellectual constructs among which socialism has been, at least for a century and a half, by far the most prominent member. Defined in such a way, utopia does not immediately reveal its bond with a specific stage of human history. Our definition has invoked so far only such attributes of human beings and their intellectual products as do not betray their time-limitations and may well be seen as accompanying human life at all times and in equal measure. Yet, utopia is a thoroughly modern phenomenon. Chad Walsh, to be sure, suggests that the entire history of utopias may be portrayed as a collection of footnotes to Plato's *Republic*:[1] this may well be so, but only in the same sense as the view that the whole of Western civilisation has done little more than elaborate and improve on seminal ideas of Plato's contemporaries and disciples. Its indebtedness to a history-long motif of human thought does not necessarily make a phenomenon ancient or timeless. And a strong case can be made for the assertion that whatever their sources of inspiration, utopias entered the historical stage as important members of the cast only after the stage had been set by a series of social and intellectual developments usually identified with the advent of modernity. I shall attempt below to single out the most significant of these phenomena, without which the advent of utopias answering the above fourfold definition would hardly be plausible.

1.   The considerable speeding up of the pace of social change rightly comes first on any imaginable list of such phenomena. The decisive threshold had been passed when change began to be ascertainable and measurable by the scale of an individual life-span; when in the course of a single individual life the change was evident

enough to demand a drastic adjustment of cognitive and moral standards. Then it was duly reflected in the new and novel sense of history as an endless chain of irreversible changes, with which the concept of progress – a development which brings change for the better – was not slow to join forces. It happened, to be sure, not before modern technology and craftsmanship took off in so spectacular a way, that it became hardly possible to defy the blatantly conspicuous evidence and insist that contemporaries knew less and possessed less skill than the ancient prodigies they wished so avidly to emulate. Only when he was sure of the 'present degree of perfection' did Francis Bacon feel prepared to 'pity the condition of mankind', observing that 'in the course of so many ages there has been so great a dearth and barrenness of arts and inventions'. It suddenly looked as if mankind had missed a chance; like Horatio Alger's poor man who has chosen to remain in his miserable condition rather than make the tiny effort of picking up the wealth waiting quietly on the pavement, Bacon's mankind had chosen to wallow in its humility by not daring to trust its own faculties: 'By far the greatest obstacle to the progress of science and to the new undertakings of new tasks . . . is found in this – that men . . . think things impossible.'[2]

What lurks behind Bacon's words is a polemic with the dominant idea of development as an effort to attain a stable and immutable state of perfection pre-ordained once and for all for each type. Bacon in fact proposed to replace the idea of perfection, which involves condemnation of all attempts to transgress the boundaries between 'ideal forms' assigned to different types, with the concept of perfectibility, which stresses movement rather than an end-point, and sets no limits to development, refusing even to discuss its supposedly final frontiers. (This distinction has been convincingly elucidated by John Passmore.)

It was only this idea of perfectibility which paved the way for utopia. Indeed, to embark on sketching the outlines of a better, though never existing social order, one has to believe that no borders are in principle unencroachable and that the ease with which even the steepest ramparts can be scaled depends in large measure, if not solely, on the boldness of human imagination. This new and emancipating belief flourished in all its numerous aspects throughout the seventeenth and the eighteenth centuries until it took solid root in the European mind to the point of becoming a part of common knowledge, the constant backcloth against which to paint innumerable utopias, ideologies, political programmes. In bringing the message home, Bacon was helped by many writers responsible for the intellectual climate of modernity. Herder was apt to express his utter amazement at the fact that of all the inhabitants of the earth men seem to be the most remote from anything which can pass for a final destination; Fontenelle emphatically rejected the view that degeneration may ever befall the human race, and manifested his unshakable conviction that no end can be envisaged to the growth of human wisdom. Condorcet joined the chorus as probably its most loquacious member and never tired of repeating that there is nothing in Nature which can possibly warrant human diffidence or the anticipation of an end to human hopes. Too sure of the ever better times that would come to stop at generalities, Condorcet attempted, with lavish splashes and lurid colours, to paint the picture of the future, giving possibly one of the first examples of 'prospective' thinking, this mixture of a forecast and a utopian call to arms: 'Our hopes regarding the future state of humanity can be reduced to these three important points: the destruction of inequality between nations; the progress of equality within one and the same nation; and, finally, the real perfecting of mankind.'[3] Granted the notorious elasticity of the last postulate, one can take this statement as containing a more or less complete list of motifs which were to be played again and again in the next century, in fact to this very day, to animate and redirect social development.

2. The breath-taking feats of natural science reduced once terrifyingly sovereign Nature to the status of a pliable, malleable stuff with which one could and should knead all kinds of useful and practicable things; and they inspired the public mind to undertake a search for similar accomplishment in the social sphere. The human environment, in its 'natural' and 'social' aspects alike, seemed passively to await the human modelling activity. It would gladly reveal its secrets to an inquiring mind, and then it would obediently lend itself to an operation aimed at bringing it closer to human need. Hence the attitude of *techne*, of manipulation, inducing deliberate and planned change, first forged in the course of wrestling with Nature, could be, without much further reflection, stretched to embrace human relations. The idea of *social engineering* was the natural product of this extrapolation, and the 'Jacobin' type, so admirably portrayed by Chad Walsh as an antonym of the

'Bourbon', became its most radical and devout preacher. The Jacobin, in Walsh's words, is 'the great theoriser, the planner, the apostle of the *tabula rasa*. He wonders why one should tinker in trivial ways with society. Why not sit down, take a long look at the social scene, mediate on first principles and draw up new blueprints?'.[4] Whatever sinister results the Jacobin blend of self-assurance and impatience may eventually bring, this view of the world has an emancipating quality since it amounts to a manifesto of the human right to shape man's own destiny and to an emphatic rejection of the authority of 'the real' and 'the realistic'. The Jacobin is the one to declare that men have history, but a history which can be consciously directed to the greater benefit of its subjects; and that man is not only perfectible, but perfectible enough to rise to the level at which he will be able to set the pattern for his own perfection.

The word 'man' used above should not imply that the Jacobin attitude (or, more broadly, a 'cultural engineering' attitude, since the Jacobin type is a blend of belief in cultural engineering plus impatience and an 'I know better' assumption) is about the individual, *qua* individual, fixing his own ends and ideal patterns entirely by himself. The Jacobin in fact shares with the Bourbon an unflattering view of the individual as an essentially wayward creature with a flair for misinterpreting his own best interests and, consequently, for being lost in the maze of historical choices. The idea which was used years later by Durkheim to build an entire theoretical system of sociology has been present in fact in European thought at least since Blaise Pascal: the idea of a crippled, wan individual overwhelmed with dangerous instincts, from which he can be rescued only by a superior, supra-individual reason. The concept of 'forcing into happiness' was in fact well entrenched in the European philosophical tradition, with God, History and Society alternating in the role of the providential force. By no means can it be associated solely with the Jacobin attitude, let alone with socialism, as the most radical of social engineering ventures. One can find, for example, a full exposition of the concept in the writings of Auguste Comte, rightly classified on the conservative side of the nineteenth-century ideological divisions: 'The end is to subordinate the satisfaction of the personal instincts to the habitual exercise of the social faculties, subjecting, at the same time, all our passions to rules imposed by an over-strengthening intelligence, with the view of identifying the individual more and more with the species.'[5]

On the strength of this quotation alone (and if nothing else were known about its author) one would not hesitate to admit Comte to the family of Jacobins. The point is that what differentiates a utopian attitude from the commonsensical mood of European thought is not the belief in *techne* and its supra-individual foundations, but the rather subtle distinction between activism and quietism, eagerness to help reason or society in hammering home the message of the ideal pattern, as opposed to the passive expectation of the millennium of reason descending upon the earth anyway, though in a piecemeal fashion and through its own slow-working, but unerring mechanisms. In the words of Richard Gerber,

> The utopian imagination cannot remain content with far-off bliss and perfection. It is characterised by an insatiable desire to pull heaven down to earth by a violent effort. It not only wants to effect a radical change here, it also wants it now, if possible. Therefore a utopia generally presents a picture of an imaginary society whose standard, in the author's opinion, ought to or might be reached by the young readers' generation within their own lifetime, or at least within a period not exceeding the time span of recorded history . . . [Therefore] the writer of social utopias of the near future has to compromise with reality in a way unknown to the creator of evolutionary myths.[6]

Of all human beings, the Utopian is perhaps the one who most faithfully approximates the Heideggerian vision of man as a creature to whom the future is primary because it is the region toward which man projects and in which he defines his own being. Slightly paraphrasing William Barrett, one can say that the Utopian 'looks ever forward, toward the open region of the future, and in so looking he takes upon himself the burden of the past (or what out of the past he selects as his inheritance) and thereby orients himself in a certain way to his present and actual situation in life'.[7] By orienting himself to the future, as the only 'pure' state cleansed thoroughly of the filth of unreason and immorality, the Utopian mind draws its moral stamina and capacity for forceful action from its knowledge of the 'true' or 'right' shape of things, and thereby disregards or challenges the possible counter-evidence furnished by the reality 'here and now'. Hence the notoriously haughty and contemptuous stance toward the resistance of the multitude, so deeply soaked in the present that they are unable or unwilling to look to the future. The fact that people do not show enough enthusiasm for their own happiness testifies to their ignorance rather than to the deficiency of the ideal.

3. 'On façonne des plantes par la culture et les hommes par l'éducation' goes the famous profession of faith of Jean Jacques Rousseau. Education is the *techne* as applied to human beings. In order to attain the right shape of things human, human beings must first of all be reshaped, brought into line with the pattern which, though it responds to the demands of reason, exists in advance only in the mind of the educator, as the plan of a bridge exists in advance in the mind of the engineer. This, of course, raises immediately the most troublesome dilemma of all social ameliora- tion: if Locke was right when he declared that men are what they are, good or evil, useful or not, by their education, then one can hardly expect that they will draw new ideas from anywhere else than from their educators. But who will educate the educators? asked Marx, bringing up-to-date Juvenal's query 'quis custodiet ipsos custodes?'. Where will the educators get their knowledge of right and wrong, truth and error? There is only one answer which could be given to this irritating question and which in fact has been given in different times and different verbalisations, which nevertheless monotonously harped on the same motif: all people are equal, but some are more equal than others; all people are educable, but some may educate themselves. European thought, developing in its modern stage under the auspices of the cult of reason, took on from the start an intrinsically elitist attitude, and this attitude furnished one of the crucial factors without which utopian thinking would not be possible.

One had to reconcile two admittedly contradictory beliefs. First, it is possible to apply *techne* to human personalities, to shape and reshape them at will; these personalities contain nothing but what has been put into them by their teachers, or by their life conditions, which unknowingly performed the role of teachers, and this applies to all people without exception. Second, people may still be lifted from their present condition and transplanted into a different world by educators who have been brought up in the same conditions and, by definition, must remain under their sway. No thinker actively committed to the cause of progress could possibly evade this antinomy. And nobody did, though the responses varied consider- ably.

One category of responses was resolutely and openly elitist. The benevolent despot; the Legislator; the Philosopher; the Scientist – all of them belonged to the family of Supermen who by dint of miraculous power, omnipotent technology or ability to wrench its secrets from History, were able to unravel and bring to their less endowed fellows the ideas which, in a sense, were 'not from this world'. This answer is still very much with us, deep down in the commonsense of the twentieth century, manifesting its presence in whatever has been left of our almost uncritical faith in the ability of science and the scientists to pave the way to a better and more congenial future: though, to be sure, it posed in this latter version a new, but equally vexing and antinomial question of how science, this completely technical-instrumental venture, can possibly tell good from evil.

The second category of answers rests on the emphatic rejection of the image of man as a passive object of education. Taking either the individual, or the society as a whole, or Reason as a supra-individual entity, as its medium, this category of answers endows existence with the capacity to transcend itself without having been set in motion by an external force; in the womb of a seemingly ossified setting new conditions mature which in fact herald its radical reconstruction. Thus capitalism breeds its own gravediggers; oppression itself stimulates forces which will eventually bring it down. Still, it can hardly do it entirely alone. The birth analogy, to be complete, requires a midwife; and she duly arrives in the attire of a social scientist, who from the radical standpoint of the oppressed penetrates the shroud of lies behind which the emancipating options are hidden, or of the New Prince, the community of dedicated guides who make up for the incurable weaknesses of the individual by the collective wisdom of revolutionary praxis. In the last resort, therefore, the same idea, constitutive of the utopian attitude, is still present, whatever the answer: people must be led into a better life, either by force, or by being shown the pattern they otherwise would not construct themselves. In either case they are not trusted with the ability to repeat the Münchhausen solution, the latter being an exclusive property of the intellectual elite.

4. The unavoidable weakness of educational efforts is that they may fail; and the notorious feature of all educators is that they tend to attribute the failure to the obstreperousness or idleness of their pupils rather than to their own frailities. In the case of the utopian thrust into the future the risk of failure is considerable, since the

twin powers of commonsense and habit are met only with the shining, but brittle, weapon of ideas. We know already that impatience is an integral constituent of the utopian attitude; we can therefore expect that the most likely reaction to the popular lack of enthusiasm for utopianists' solicitations will be a vigorous condemnation of the dumbness and stupor of the multitude. The same people whom the utopian programme was bound to make happy will soon be declared responsible for the programme's failure to materialise promptly enough.

Once again, the image of the multitude as a sluggish, inert mass, wallowing in misery, but refusing to be stood on its own feet, is the verso of the elitarian coin and therefore inextricably linked with the modern cult of reason. At worst the masses were denounced as the strongholds of the retrograde and obscurantist forces which held society back; at best they were pitied as lame creatures, unable to move, unless helped by crutches supplied by the sages. According to de Tocqueville's testimony, the people-loving philosophers of the French Enlightenment 'despised the public almost as heartily as they despised the Deity'.[8] John Passmore recently amplified this testimony by collecting an impressive array of statements which expose the philosophers' zeal in attributing the sluggishness of human progress to people's inactivity and cowardice. Thus, according to Diderot, 'the people are the most foolish and the most wicked of all men'. For d'Alembert, the multitude was 'ignorant and stupefied' and 'incapable of strong and generous actions'. Nothing was left for Condillac but to compare 'the people' to 'a ferocious animal'.[9] As to the next period of European intellectual history, one is bound to accept Crane Brinton's estimate: 'Ever since the failure of the French Revolution to live up to the hopes they had put in it, many writers, artists, and musicians of great distinction and influence have found the main obstacle to the good society in the bourgeois, the Philistine, the *homme moyen sensuel*, the Babbitts, the masses'.[10] The vocabulary has been changed to adjust it to a more populist mood of the late nineteenth century, but the object of contempt and angry accusations remains the same as before; the culturally retarded masses who refuse to be enlightened. The likelihood of a 'bewildered disappointment' with the masses became particularly great when, in Stuart Hughes's words, 'the intellectual leaders began to identify themselves with democracy or socialism and sought virtue in the cultural pursuits of the common man'.[11] In Marx's mind, to be sure, and to an even greater extent in Lenin's, the image of the working class as the fearless and never erring giant about to pull down the rotten structure of bourgeois society coexisted with a hardly flattering picture of specific workers and actual labour organisations as pedestrian, opportunist, and eager to play the bourgeois game according to bourgeois rules. The second picture was invoked whenever the first failed to materialise.

The castigation of *kosnoie bolshinstvo* (Lenin) is a device which may heal the psychic wound inflicted by an acute cognitive dissonance; but it will hardly push much further the cause of the desired social reconstruction. The more practical remedy would be if the advocates of social reconstruction tried to by-pass the obstacle (the expedient which in fact they soon began to try) by attempting to 'short-circuit'[12] the road to the perfect society. Since, as Eric Hobsbawm once described this attitude, the masses will certainly appreciate liberation but would hardly lift a finger to help in bringing it about, somebody is bound to do the job for them. Hence the idea of a minority revolution, limited in its initial and decisive act to a purely political task of capturing the centres of power, and then employing the captured assets to redirect the whole process of education so as to breed a new race of people fit to live in and to sustain the perfect society.

It has escaped my memory who made the observation that the phrase 'minority revolution' contains one word which is redundant, since a majority may do without a revolution. This observation may be profound and witty, but the ever-widening current in utopian thought from Babeuf through Blanqui to Tkachev, Lavrov and Lenin (the close intellectual link between the last three has recently been convincingly brought to our attention[13]) insisted on the concept of a revolution which may be brought about, fought and won specifically by a minority, as an alternative to a protracted and probably futile wait for the conversion of the majority.

The word 'minority', therefore, whether redundant or not, bore an important additional significance, conveying a specific philosophy of social change and a specific way out of the irritating cognitive dissonance with which the educational antinomy left the champions of the better society. It was Blaise Pascal who singled out habit and diversion as the two expedients men universally employ to shirk looking their frightening predicament in the face; and it was only reasonable to expect that these would be the most likely responses of the common man to the conditions from which the utopians wanted to liberate him. Elaborate sociological theories were developed to show how a social system sustains itself by stretching over its essential patterns a protective net of habit and diversion, surrounding the common man with a multitude of petty barriers and warning signs, as well as by hosts of paltry rewards complete with a morality which hails the virtues of these rewards. In this way society is seen as generating a situation in which obedience becomes normal and in a sense self-fulfilling, while dissent becomes both aberrant and heroic. Whoever is bent on a drastic reform of the societal pattern would therefore be advised not to expect much from spontaneous processes developing within this pattern; if anything, they will tend to reproduce the same pattern again and again. Once more the partisans of utopia face the Münchhausen dilemma; and they single out coercion as the required leverage which may lift men from the quagmire of habitual abasement.

To be sure, the word coercion stands here, at least in its first appearance in the argument, for an out-of-the-ordinary agent able to stall the monotonous self-regeneration of the current societal pattern; in this sense it belongs in one family with Weberian 'charisma' or the 'cultural diffusion' of anthropologists. Their shared feature is their relative 'externality' to the existing system, and, therefore, their essential inexplicability and unpredictability from within the cognitive perspective determined by the system itself. Coercion, before it is defined in phenomenal terms, stands for a factor potent enough to counterbalance and topple the bulwarks of reality, to break its 'regularity'. As such it may be, and must be, operated by the few, who act as heralds and vanguard of the future. The revolution, as a technical device, is logically derivative; it designates the means of bringing forth a situation in which this exertion of power in the name of the reshaping of society will be possible.

But coercion occupies an exceptional place in the aforementioned family, in so far as it is seen as a factor constantly present in any 'normal' society and continually employed to strengthen and diffuse whatever patterns are regarded as essential for the survival of the current system. At the same time coercion is a factor which, in a sense, is 'in', but not necessarily 'of' the system; it is, so to speak, a detachable part. Or, one might say, it is a tool which can be used as much for the benefit of the system as to its detriment, depending on the intention of those who wield it. This extraordinary role allotted to coercion in the modern philosophy of societal change has recently been admirably expressed by Barrington Moore Jr. In his words, both cultural and social continuity

> have to be recreated anew in each generation. To maintain and transmit a value system, human beings are punched, bullied, sent to jail, thrown into concentration camps, cajoled, bribed, made into heroes, encouraged to read newspapers, stood up against a wall and shot, and sometimes even taught sociology. . . . The costs of moderation have been at least as atrocious as those of revolution, perhaps a great deal more. . . . The use of force by the oppressed against their former master has been the object of nearly universal condemnation. Meanwhile the day-to-day repression of 'normal' society hovers dimly in the background of most history books.[14]

The point is that when confronted with coercive power human beings assent to being cajoled and bribed and taught sociology rather than being stood up against the wall and shot. It does matter, therefore, who holds the power and for what purpose. The revolutionary transfer of power may set the society on a new road and secure the dissemination and sustenance of a new value system. Being an intense dramatisation of the power game, the revolution means a spectacular condensation of its usual costs. This optical illusion, however, which is the sole basis for the moral objections levelled against revolutionaries, will vanish (or so it is said) if only one counts the human costs of coercion necessary to keep the revolution off.

5.　It is only recently that we have begun to realise the extent to which modern thought is prompted by the cravings for order. To be sure, it has frequently been observed that the literary utopias were obsessed with painting their ideal worlds tidy, neat and regular in the extreme. Their authors, it has been pointed out, were particularly keen on using symbols which, in the public mind, approach most closely the image of a perfect orderliness. Lewis Mumford has noted that in most literary utopias islands are circular, buildings rectangular, streets straight, etc.;[15] Chad Walsh observed that 'the favourite utopian art is architecture. Characteristically it is massive, functional, glistening and clean. Cities look as though they were laid out with straight-edge and T-square. . . . In the utopias there is often a tidying-up of both the natural and human scene, with much emphasis on spick-and-span. . . .'[16] But precisely this obsession of the draftsmen of utopias was more often than not singled out as the paramount evidence of the intrinsic marginality of utopian thinking; they seemed, indeed, wide of the mark in a world perceived as relishing the flux of constant change and adventure.

But circles and rectangles, particularly in architecture, can be read as symbols for another motive as well. The concept of architecture can well be conceived as the foremost symbol of the human multi-faceted effort to impose man-measured regularity and consistency on inhospitable nature; man's success in this matter, moreover, is proportionate to his success in sneaking nature's secrets and turning them to his own advantage. Architecture, therefore, is coterminous with the thoroughly modern, scientific attitude; after all, the unlimited increase of human skill in subduing nature and harnessing it to human needs is what science is all about. The very project of science, as it has been gradually advanced in the modern age, starts from an attitude which in the last analysis amounts to defining the human life-world as natural, i.e. as consisting of objects of human planful activity, and positing the fruition of this activity as simply a problem of appropriate technical skill. As to the ends of such activity it has been assumed, at least since Francis Bacon's time, that they are closely related to the substitution of a human-made and human-desired order for the natural one, which obviously was not cut to the measure of human needs. Far from being an alien body within modern thought, the utopian quest for order merely condenses and intensifies the attitude which is riveted into the practice of modern science; it lays bare what science itself aims at but would rather not make explicit lest its keenly cultivated ideal of value-neutrality becomes vulnerable. By locating the difference between the utopian and the scientific attitude in the domain of order, the critics in fact misinterpreted the actual discrepancy; utopias and science diverge in their view as to who may, and who may not, fix the ends of human technical efforts. Utopians would harness the science-generated instrumental capacity to the chariot of a specific order they deem the best; scientists would be wary of committing themselves to a specific kind of order (if not, they write utopias, as Skinner did). They insist instead on limiting their programme to the design and polishing of tools that are meant to introduce more human order into the chaos of nature. And they maintain that the efficiency of these tools is largely independent of the kind of values which may mark off any concrete order from all other conceivable specimens of the kind.

The advent of modernity destroyed the 'immediate', 'transparent' (hence perceived as natural) order of the pre-industrial, mostly rural society. The kind of order buttressed by habit and repetition, from which pre-industrial man drew his emotional security as well as his illusion of complete mastery over his own life, was no more. It was therefore apparent that any order which might eventually come to replace it must be an artificial creation of planners, much as the former order seemed to have emerged 'naturally' or to have been ordained by a superhuman power. From being a part and parcel of the natural world, the human order moved to the region of *techne*. Whatever the ideal of order upheld by this or that group afflicted with uncertainty and insecurity, it has been beyond discussion that the order would not come unless 'organised' or 'administered'. In this respect, as in so many others, utopian thinking has merely been faithful to the popular mood of modern times.

Whenever blueprints of a future order are drafted, two attitudes are possible. First, one may see the current disruption of orderly life as a temporary malaise inflicted by an inept or morally corrupt administration of human affairs. One is ready to embrace all the powerful factors which keep the present system going, considering them as an undetachable part of a welcome progress or 'leap forward'; but one would organise them in a different way, hoping that at the end of the road, or just ahead, a new, never tried, but better order is waiting. Second, one may perceive the current disorder as a permanent and unavoidable effect of the original deviation from a simpler, but more humane way of life. One would therefore reject all the trappings of the new system, together with the very notion of progress, expecting nothing but more evil from letting loose the factors which operate it; not trusting the yet unexplored solutions, one would feel like returning to what can be portrayed as the 'natural' organisation of human affairs, and to do it one would willingly surrender the problematical benefits offered by the existing system.

It is easy to trace both attitudes in modern utopian thinking. Numerous future-planners, from Saint-Simon through Marx to Bellamy, enthusiastically embraced modern industry and technology as the surest warranty of the impending millennium. Most of them detested the misuse to which the newly discovered tremendous powers of man are put when mismanaged. But they did see the departure from pre-industrial life as irreversible and final, and, moreover, welcomed it wholeheartedly. On this point there were relatively minor differences between thinkers politically as far apart as Jeremy Bentham and Karl Marx; the first saw in the modern factory (which he artlessly viewed as coterminous with prison) a ready-made pattern for a perfect social order; the second defined socialism as a modern factory minus capitalists. The tacit agreement was indeed so broad and unconditional that Marx felt no reservations about naming Saint-Simon, that troubadour of the ascending capitalist class, among his predecessors and sources of inspiration – even among the first socialists. This agreement among a large number of utopian thinkers reflected a more or less unified common-sense attitude, which quickly developed an intense dislike and suspicion of humanitarian and aesthetic, *Schöngeist*-like objections to technological progress.[17]

On the other hand, nostalgic dreams about the lost pre-industrial paradise never stopped for a moment, even if the life-world generated by the emerging and triumphant capitalist market carried little to lend them even a semblance of realism, or, as it were, to make them attractive enough to inflame the public imagination. Their intellectual impact was in fact much wider than one would think when scanning the 'surface' message of utopias alone. Even the most ardent preachers of the new industrial world must have drawn their definition of order, as a safe and predictable situation founded on the regularity and recurrence of human conduct, from the living memory of the past, since it was never demonstrated by the system currently in existence. One may legitimately ask whether any blueprint for the future can ever be produced entirely from scratch, without the author's helping himself generously to the stock of collective memories and accessible experiences. Hence the frequently noted tenuousness of the line dividing 'prospective' from 'retrospective' utopias, enthusiasm for progress from a conservative nostalgia. The real dividing line runs between the preachers of greater complexity and the admirers of simplicity (in the latter case it is, by definition, always a 'return' to simplicity).

Simplicity in the modern context meant invariably a *Gemeinschaft*-like dimension of human life, achievable only through dislodging or weakening the integration-sustaining institutions of the greater society. It is assumed that when all important human relations are face-to-face (which is possible only if the web of human dependencies generated by work, communication and power is cut to a community size) all the strain attached to the structural incertitude will be removed, thanks to the restored 'immediacy' and 'translucence' of

the individual life-world. The craftsmen faced with the imminent
loss of independence will side with Proudhon and his syndicalist offshoots in their praise of the untarnished virtues of a small-scale,
self-governing community of individual producers. Almost the entire
middle class of the most affluent country in the world will follow, at
least to the polling booths, a sheep farmer who extols the pastoral
beauty and the moral vigour of the countryside. The offspring of
affluent families in another thriving super-industrial country will
listen attentively to the message that 'participatory democracy
postulates low energy technology'.[18] Other offspring of the same
families will abandon anxieties and tensions which their parents
would like them to inherit and will try to taste the primitive charm
of tribal life.

To be sure, the 'come-back' rationale of the 'great simplification'
is an optical illusion. It is certainly not the rural community of
sweating Russian peasants, however idealised, to which the dreamers
of simplification would like to 'return'; nor the cruel, inhospitable
world of primitive hunters and gatherers. It is Rabelais's Thelema
rather than any other ready-made pattern which provides today
the source of inspiration. As in the upper-middle-class 'idolum of
the Country House',[19] the crux of the matter is now passive enjoyment rather than hard work. It is true that the simplifiers renounce
possession along with hard work; but they merely substitute accumulation of events for the accumulation of things, while retaining
the hedonistic ideal of gourmandism and sensual thrill as the
supreme canon of judgement. Perhaps the only factor limiting the
love of enjoyment is the hatred of the puritan achievement.

One is tempted to associate utopias of simplification with the
middle classes of modern society – those who neither rose so high
as to treat the powerful modern state as a convenient tool of self-
enhancement, nor were cast so low as to count on publicly administered justice as their only hope. If they had risen they would
probably not have indulged in utopian dreams; if they had fallen
they would probably have opted for as much complexity as might
have been necessary to guarantee their survival. Not every law pays
heed to the need of the weaker; but the lack of law certainly makes
the strong even stronger. It is the weakest and the wretched of the
earth who are most likely to dream of a power strong and
determined enough to intervene on their behalf in a struggle in
which the 'natural' deal left them with a hopeless hand.

We have seen that in its notorious yearning for order, as in its other traits, utopian thinking is not alien to the modern world. It shares its attitude with science, this law-giver and chief referee of the modern intellectual game; though it does not recognise the division between 'pure' and 'practical' reason which science would so meticulously observe. Here at last we come across one respect in which the utopian attitude obviously takes issue with science.

It is, to be sure, a ramified issue, with many dimensions which can be and frequently are discussed separately, but all these contentious points can be traced back to one central disagreement: utopian thinking defies science's reduction of man, in the process of cognition, to a purely epistemological and contemplative entity. It defies this reduction by legitimising the status of 'the possible' in valid knowledge.

The nearest the scientific mentality comes to this category is in its concern with 'the probable'. But these two categories, sometimes unjustly confused in everyday discourse, enjoy very different and hardly reconcilable existential modalities. The judgement which refers to the probability of an event conveys no information about the occurrence of the event, but precisely about the probability of the occurrence. The statement stands or falls by the verification of probability, not by the materialisation or non-materialisation of the event in question at a specific time or a specific place; if this were not the case, science would lack means to deal with the phenomenon of probability, since it is able to deal only with *facta*, not with *futura*.[20] Probability belongs to the realm of *facta*, to the realm of events which have already taken place, which can be relished or regretted, but cannot be changed; events in relation to which men have neither will nor liberty of action, neither power nor influence. Precisely because of this quality of *facta*, which puts men in a position of passive contemplation, they are 'knowable' in the scientific way. And so is probability; it belongs to *facta*, it 'has already been done', it exists in a tangible way, here and now, within the reality open to our scrutiny and subject to verification. Any statement about probability refers to the data we already possess and can be verified or denied with reference to them; it contains information about the present state of our knowledge.

The position is entirely different in the case of possibility, as I propose to define it. I am aware that the definition which follows is not the only one which can be conceived. Indeed, time and again one can find statements to the effect that probability is a measure of possibility; that it belongs to one and the same class of concepts.

B

According to this usage we are forced to settle for possibility whenever we are not able to express it mathematically (to measure it)
and thereby portray it as probability. Or science may take the
probability of an event as only a 'possibility' whenever it does not
know of any law, or does not possess any previous knowledge,
which may contradict its occurrence. In the first case, possibility is
nothing but a weaker version of probability; in the second, it is a
purely negative notion, a notion 'not-yet-rejected'. Because of this
usage of the term, our appropriating it for another concept may
engender some confusion. The only justification for still insisting
on it is our conviction that depriving 'possibility' of its separate
modality has been an unfortunate by-product of the positivistic
dominance over modern self-consciousness. It has been, indeed, one
of the many steps toward the final, yet spurious reconcilation between the individual and the reality which controls him; or toward
acceptance, as natural, of what is merely historical.

Now the category of the possible, which could not be absorbed
by science (in Emile Meyerson's words, 'reason has only one means
of accounting for what does not come from itself, and that is to
reduce it to nothingness'[21]), stands for an event, not for the probability of its occurrence. It signifies an event which has not yet
happened, and whose future occurrence cannot in principle be
established on the basis of data about *facta*; not because the
accessible knowledge is insufficient, but because the very naming
of the possibility, as well as the ensuing human activity, are among
the decisive factors which will eventually determine whether the
possibility ever materialises. As Leszek Kołakowski has put it
succinctly, the existence of the utopia as utopia is the undeniable
condition for the possibility that the utopia may cease to be
utopia. Possibility in this sense is a category which applies solely
to the human world, namely the world of events on which informed
human volition may exercise a determining influence.

The important distinction between objects which we approach as
natural, and that part of human existence which resists such an
approach, is the distinction between 'being', as an attribute ascrib-
able to Nature, and 'becoming', as a uniquely human way of being-
in-the-world. It belongs to the essence of human existence that it is
ever unfinished and inconclusive, open toward the future, lived,
evaluated and revised under the auspices of events which exist so
far only ideally, as an end of human effort, as a desirable state,
as an ideal pattern, as a nostalgia, a plan, a dream, a threat, a hope,

or a danger. All these events belong to the class of possibilities, which are not present in daily reality in any other way but ideally, and therefore come into existence the moment they reach the level of consciousness, are named and made into a subject of interhuman communication. The unique significance of this class consists in the fact that it, and it alone, creates a chance for new forms to enter human reality, and for the human reality itself to unfold dynamically its inner potentialities. The life-world in which human life activity takes place embraces the class of possibilities. Without them it would certainly be incomplete as a human world; in fact, it would not be a human world any more. It is only reasonable to postulate that this life-world, complete with the class of possibilities, should be taken as the appropriate frame of reference in which to inscribe analytically, to classify and understand human life activity.

If, however, we abide by this postulate, a number of important revisions of notions whose meaning has so far been determined solely by their intra-scientific usage will become imperative. The most obvious revision will be that of the concept of rationality, somewhat inhumanly reduced to what can be measured, exactly and *hic et nunc*, by reference to *facta* alone, instead of looking up to the genuinely human level of historical possibility. Utopia, which spells out the range of possibilities, draws a horizon for the current human reality, says Bloch. The scientific attitude, which would restrict the field of permitted knowledge to that part of the human world which has already been traversed and left behind, conveys a distorted, since impoverished, picture of the actual field in which human perception, ratiocination and decision-making take place. Men see their situation in terms of its distance from the horizon which exists only as a possibility; and our analysis of the degree of rationality in their behaviour will not fully recognise the role played by reason unless we refer the concept of rationality to the continual effort to diminish the gap which divides the reality at hand from another, possible reality, still eluding the grasp of instrumentally oriented science. This approach, apparently defying the most essential canons of science, is more akin to the mode of human existence, which is intrinsically critical, continuously 'transcending without transcendence' (Bloch); and 'by placing itself on a normative standpoint, distantiates itself from the actual situation and views the existing achievement as relative'.[22] Utopia in particular, and the category of possibility in general, seem to reflect correctly this description of the human modality. As Theodore

Adorno put it, society can become 'problematic' (i.e. an object of intellectual and practical criticism), only if people can conceive of one which is different from it.[23]

If we only agree on this meaning of the possible we shall see the number of proclaimed utopias and the intensity of popular commitment to them not as a sign of growing irrationalism and a departure from the rule of reason, but as a measure of the vitality and creative vigour of the epoch. It is the obverse situation, as Martin Plattel recently remarked – the situation of acute shortage of utopias and widespread disenchantment with the utopias trusted the other day – which paves the way to the ascendency of irrationalism and obscurantism. The lack of utopia creates a void, an opaque, bottomless abyss, in place of a smooth extension of the present. It is the dread of this intellectually unfathomable void that leads people to escape into the mystique of irrationalism. It is in a reality lacking any horizon that the would-be Lenins of the West 'see themselves reduced to leaders of small cults or, worse yet, transformed into parliamentarians or academicians'.[24]

This somewhat lengthy digression seemed necessary to explain why I regard the analytical framework of utopia as particularly germane to the sociological analysis of modern socialism. Socialism has been, and to some extent still is, *the* utopia of the modern epoch. It has been, to quote Tom Bottomore, the counter-culture of capitalist society, if by counter-culture one means the fulcrum on which the emancipatory criticism-through-relativisation of the current reality rests. It should be clear by now that to classify socialism as a utopia does not belittle its immense historical significance. On the contrary, I hope to show in the following chapters that whatever inspiring power socialism can justly boast is drawn from its utopian status. Socialism shares with all other utopias the unpleasant quality of retaining its fertility only in so far as it resides in the realm of the possible. The moment it is proclaimed as accomplished, as empirical reality, it loses its creative power; far from inflaming human imagination, it puts on the agenda in turn an acute demand for a new horizon, distant enough to transcend and relativise its own limitations. By being perceived as realised, says Richard Gerber, an ideal ceases to be ideal.[25] The two centuries of modern socialism's history extend from its majestic advent in the attire of utopia to the incapacitation arising from its alleged realisation.

The one remaining, and probably most contentious, question is how, and to what extent, a study which takes the category of utopia, or the 'possible', for its analytical framework, can be regarded as sociological. The obvious way of approaching the phenomenon of utopia sociologically is to treat it as an 'object', as an objectified artefact of human thinking, perhaps more aberrant than other specimens of the kind, but still rightfully a member of the class which sociology knows well how to investigate, by relating it to the 'social background', statistically assessing its distribution, and formulating a number of hypotheses as to its possible influence on human behaviour. This is not, however, the way in which I propose to approach the problem. I intend to investigate the socialist utopia as an alternative social reality, which differs from the historically accomplished one by its specific existential modality: that of possibility. I am in full agreement with Robert Nisbet when he says that 'at first sight, utopianism and genuine social science may seem to be incompatible. But they are not. Utopianism is compatible with everything but determinism, and it can as easily be the over-all context of social science as can any other creative vision'.[26]

3

The Historical Location of Socialism

Modernity is, admittedly, a multi-faceted phenomenon which valiantly resists clear-cut definitions. It has been widely accepted that the phenomenon is intimately related to the 'technological revolution', to the drastic thickening of the artificial intermediary sphere stretching *between* Man and Nature, often articulated as a dramatic strengthening of the human ascendancy *over* Nature. At the same time, however, it is agreed that the phenomenon is not reducible to the technological explosion. Modernity is also a social and psychological phenomenon; its advent means momentous changes in the social system as well as in the set of conditions in which human action takes place. One can only surmise that however the advent of modernity affects the dimensions and the content of yearnings and utopias, the impact is mediated by these latter phenomena more than by anything else. As a background and a source of inspiration for human ideals, modernity means, above all, a modern network of human relations.

In what is perhaps the best recent example of the Weberian ideal-type method in action, Reinhard Bendix went a long way toward elucidating major features of this network. Two processes, Bendix suggests, contributed more than anything else to the final shape which modern society has assumed: the first was the rising pre-eminence of 'impersonalism' as the paramount principle regulating the way in which individuals were pinioned into the network of socially defined roles and behavioural patterns; the second was the advent of 'plebiscitarianism', as – simultaneously – the authority's working rule and the keynote of its legitimation.[1]

'Impersonalism' comes to replace the paternalistic relationship between patron and client. To use Parsonian language, the latter may be described as subject to the patterns of universalism and specificity, in contradistinction to the particularism and diffuseness of the former. The non-modern patterns of human relations are thoroughly particularised and widely different from one pair of individuals to another; they are likewise diffuse, tending to embrace the totality of life-processes in which both individuals are entangled. Both attributes disappear with the advent of modernity, to be replaced by their opposites. Modernity begins, says Bendix, with the codification of rights and duties of a 'citizen', an individual *qua homo politicus*, i.e. as a member of the 'polis', the politically organised society. On the other hand, this 'individual' enters the society, or is of any interest to society, only in respect of those traits which have undergone this process of 'codification', have been standardised and subjected to a set of uniform rules. The individual, as defined and moulded by the modern network, is thereby charged with an irreducible paradox; his 'individuality' has been achieved at the expense of all and any of his idiosyncratic, purely personal and genuinely unique predicates, which constitute him as a separate, irreplaceable and unrepeatable being. This peculiar individuality is anonymous and faceless, pared to the bones of pure universality, swept clean of anything idiomatic and distinctive, of any personal faculty which may thwart his complete mapping into another 'individual'. This is not to say, to be sure, that the human denizens of the modern age are really like this; but it does mean that they are admitted into modernity in this capacity only. Modern society has, admittedly, no use for unstandardised human traits; these, classified as the realm of the subjective, are declared socially irrelevant in so far as they do not interfere with the codified domain. At the same time they delimit the sphere of individual freedom; the non-interference of society is ultimately founded on its programmatic indifference to anything which eludes the supra-individual ordering, or has been deliberately exempted from it.

The principle of impersonalism not only delimits the social essence of the individual; it is operative in generating a life-space congenial to and consonant with such delimited individuals. The realm enveloping the social existence of the individual likewise consists of averaged, impersonal, faceless and hence quantifiable individuals. It can be handled effectively, assessed and evaluated, in purely numerical terms; thanks to the prior qualitative reduction of its inhabitants, it is indeed quantifiable and therefore amenable to management ruled by the economics of rationality. Again, this does not mean that the human life-process in the modern milieu boils down to a series of rational calculations and choices; but it does mean that only this series is recognised as socially relevant, and thereby socially protected and attended to. The residue, however immense and subjectively important it may be, is left in what, from the social perspective, may as well remain forever the penumbra of 'the private'. Vast areas of human life – indeed, its most intimate, passionately lived and emotion-saturated areas – have been proclaimed 'off limits' for the sake of the regularity, and therefore certainty and predictability, of the societally processed nucleus.

A rather important remark is in order here. At least since the famous distinction made by Sir Henry Maine in the nineteenth century, the dichotomy of impersonalism-particularism tends to be analysed in 'either-or' terms, Bendix's study being no exception. This approach is entirely warranted in so far as we are interested solely in the texture of the social structure, the web of interhuman dependencies, which open, limit, and condition the individual's access to socially valued goods. But the social structure in this sense does not pre-empt the totality of the individual life-world. I wonder whether it would not be better to speak of a 'topping' of the traditional life-world, in modern times, with an impersonal structure of the greater society, rather than of the substitution of this structure for the old, particularised one. A very large part of the life-world still remains heavily 'particularised', densely packed with face-to-face, multi-faceted relations and apparently open to meaning-negotiating initiatives; it is still 'free' in the latter sense, its freedom having been given a new, deeper dimension and been made particularly conspicuous by contrast with the new domain of the thoroughly standardised, prefigured relations. The 'freedom' which prevails in this part of the life-world should be understood only in these comparative terms. Otherwise it becomes an illusion, since the sector of the life-world now under discussion, having been abandoned by the 'impersonal' control of the greater society, is still kept under tight control by the community (defined as the group able to hold its members under a face-to-face, immediate, and personal control). The activity of meaning-negotiating never takes off from a zero-point; in each case the cards have already been distributed and the hands are not even, while the rules of the game itself are hardly open to negotiation by the current players. The last decade showed what the consequences of this distorted perspective may be; the so-called 'youth revolt' tried in fact to shake off the constraints imposed on the community level, while being con-

vinced that it fought the 'impersonal society'. Its success in subduing the power of community control was naturally proportionate
to the widening of the sphere of impersonal regulation and interference (through new laws which introduced the 'greater society'
into areas where it had traditionally been indifferent).

Plebiscitarianism – the second of Bendix's two parameters of
modernity – consists in the inclusion of the masses in the political
process. They now become 'citizens' of the state instead of subjects
of a prince. Their collective will now becomes the seat of sovereignty
and its supreme legitimation. Quantity is substituted for quality,
numerical power for wisdom, interests for inalienable rights, accomplishment for properties. The substitution, to be sure, is perceived only too often as an improvement on the inductive definitions
of old and immutable values, rather than as one value taking the
place of another. Thus quantity is considered the best measure of
quality, the number of supporters a true index of the wisdom of a
decision, pursuit of interest the least alienable of human rights.
From the vantage-point of their sociological content, however, the
change in values is enormous and radical. The paramount novelty
is the sheer notion of the masses as the 'flesh' of the body politic.
The passage from the patrimonial ruler to the rule of the masses is
not to be seen merely as a widening of the ruling group, as a substitution of the many for the few. The masses turned citizens do not
take over the former rulers' faculty of entering the field of politics
as socially identifiable persons. Only when they have undergone
and completed the process of impersonalisation can the subjects of
a patrimonial ruler re-emerge as the masses looming large in the
modern idiom of authority. The masses are not a collection of
specific, qualitatively distinct persons, complete with their multi-
faceted qualities, needs, and interests. They are describable and
intelligible in quantitative terms only, which is possible only on the
assumption of their complete comparability and exchangeability in
their role of citizens. It is thanks to this reduction, accomplished
by the modern notion of citizenship, that public opinion can boil
down to the computation of statistical distributions and democracy
can be measured by a crudely arithmetical yardstick of numerical
majority. The citizens are equal in so far as they are indistinguishable; whatever makes them different from each other is simply left
outside the realm of politics and the interests of the body politic.
So we see that, within the modern idiom, impersonalism and
plebiscitarianism are not just parallel processes which happen to

B*

occur simultaneously; they complement, validate and support each other, and can be seen as two sides of the same coin. The impersonal equality of individuals as citizens can generate, or be squared with, only a plebiscitarian type of body politic; and plebiscitarianism cannot assure, or account for, any but an impersonal type of equality, i.e. equality contained in the citizen role.

However, this is not the end of the story. Plebiscitarianism does not only disregard the differentiation of citizens beyond the sphere of citizenship proper. It also works on the assumption that non-political inequality does not affect the role of the citizen; that citizens somehow shake off their non-political bonds at the threshold of the body politic. Having theoretically separated the sector of citizenship from the totality of the individual's status, the plebiscitarian legitimation conceives its conceptual feat as an operation on social reality; it is, indeed, founded on the belief that an individual can enjoy his equal political rights while remaining unequal in spheres other than the political.

It is true that the roots of inequality, in the modern society which has gradually emerged from the lasting victories and temporary setbacks of the French Revolution, were not political. They were dug deep into the network of economic dependencies and the web of communication which constituted the civil society of the era. But it is true as well that with these bases of self-perpetuating inequality left intact, the political equality of plebiscitarianism must have remained a purely formal legal category. It was precisely in this form that the ideal of equality had been adopted by the dominant, liberal culture of the capitalist brand of the modern society. And it was precisely in this form that the ideal of purely political equality had been challenged and rejected by its socialist counter-culture. The emphatic refusal to accept the notion of equality as limited to the political sphere alone, the insistence on the importance of the numerous links with other spheres which render political equality void if other inequalities are left intact, and the determined desire to extend the ideal of equality beyond the domain of *homo politicus* were to remain the only cultural postulates shared by all shades of the socialist counter-culture.

In this sense, the socialist counter-culture was a continuation of the liberal-capitalist culture as well as its rejection. Already in 1890, Bebel publicly acknowledged socialism's indebtness: no one had done more than the liberals to awaken the yearning for equality among the people. The liberal notion of political democracy was the first form in which the vision and the realism of equality had been brought to the mind of the common man and kindled his imagination. 'Patiently endured so long as it seemed beyond redress,' wrote de Tocqueville, 'a grievance comes to appear intolerable once the possibility of removing it crosses men's minds.'[2] In one fell swoop the capitalist cultural revolution disposed of the two pillars of the pre-modern belief system: that human inequality is beyond challenge and dispute; and that it is pre-ordained, and therefore cannot be changed by men. In this myth-destroying activity the liberal-capitalist culture soon reached the point of no return; from now on it was an unquestionable belief that inequality is unjust, man-made, and therefore subject to man's action. What remained to be done by the socialist counter-culture was to draw conclusions the liberal ideology could not, and did not wish to draw: that what had been done in politics could and should be repeated in the other spheres of human deprivation. As one of the delegates of the South German People's Party expressed it at a conference in 1868, 'Democracy must become social democracy if it honestly wants to be democracy'.[3]

Socialism may be seen, so to speak, as a radical but logical extension of capitalist liberalism. It was not, however, only an extension of the critical aspect of liberalism; it involved, simultaneously, an emphatic rejection of its positive side. Liberalism saw the equality of citizenship as the foundation and guarantee of the individual's freedom, i.e. his freedom to be unequal in other spheres than the political. Socialism, on the contrary, considered the establishment of political equality as a means and a first step to the incorporation of the totality of individual life into a community of equal men. In other words, liberalism saw the community as a major obstacle on the way to individual freedom and understood the body politic as the only desirable form of supra-individual integration on the new societal level, with citizenship as the only integrating link; while socialism aimed at the reconstruction of a community-type integration on the societal level.

Throughout the two centuries of socialist thought we find the two threads – the radical version of critical liberalism and the rejection of positive liberalism – closely knit together. The words which Jean Jacques Rousseau put into the mouth of Pliny speaking to Trajan, 'If we have a prince, it is in order that he keeps us from having a master', were to remain the leitmotiv of the socialist concept of the body-politic, but pushed well beyond the boundary of the liberal interpretation. This boundary was drawn by the idea that masters are born, as Morelly noted already in 1755, not of the usurpation of power, but of resources which precede all politics and whose usurpation alone can make men power-hungry. The legislators, Morelly was eager to make clear, support the masters rather than creating them; they do it by allowing for the usurpation of resources and defending the ensuing situation. The major disaster took place at the moment when the resources, which should belong in common to all humanity, had been usurped; the disaster consisted in breaking the primary link of sociability. Thus destruction of community and inequality became one; and the rebirth of community and the establishment of more than just political equality become one again.

It was left to Gracchus Babeuf to cross the t's and dot the i's. In the history of socialism the role of Babeuf is unique and perhaps decisive. It was he who finally brought together and blended two traditions which had previously developed independently of each other: the tradition of socialism as an abstract moral principle, as a verdict of reason, the heritage of Plato, Morus and Campanella, and the plebeian tradition of revolt against injustice, reaching back into antiquity to the brothers from whom Babeuf borrowed his assumed first name. In a sense, the role of Babeuf for socialism may be compared to the role of Galileo for science; it was Galileo who married the philosophers' rationalist tradition of logical truth with the plebeian tradition of craftsmen's empiricism and *techne*.

Babeuf articulated, as a separate and consistent system of ideas, the utopia of the sansculottes which strove, in the course of the French Revolution, to cut the umbilical cord tying it to bourgeois individualist egalitarianism. While the inchoate capitalist culture sought in political equality a bulwark to protect an unqualified and unchecked individualism, the sansculottes looked toward the state as an active power to be used for curbing and controlling the individual in the name of the community. Both currents could be accommodated in one river-bed until the river passed the point of the equality of political rights. Beyond this point, however, a bifurcation was inevitable.

In Babeuf's epoch-making statement in the *Manifesto of the Equals* (1796) the realisation of this inevitability was for the first time made explicit. The French Revolution was only a prelude to another revolution. The Declaration of the Rights of Man and the Citizen was a step in the right direction, but by no means the end of the process; in fact, merely its beginning. The equality which the Declaration proclaimed 'we must have in our midst, under the roof of our houses'. How to bring it there? By placing on the agenda a new revolutionary goal, on which the Declaration is mute, and which, in fact, flies in the face of the interpretation of equality which the Declaration took for granted: the goal of doing away with the terrible contrasts between rich and poor, masters and servants. Unless this goal is attained, equality will remain nothing but a fine and sterile fiction of the law.

Babeuf would elaborate further on these ideas a year later, when defending himself during the Vendôme trial. It was there that the concept of 'the welfare of men' was first brought to the fore, as Babeuf himself was apt to stress, as 'a new idea in Europe'. What followed was already a gigantic step beyond even the most generous promises of bourgeois equality: the existence of an unfortunate or a poor man in the state is not to be endured. 'The unfortunate are the powers of the earth; they have the right to speak as masters to the governments that neglect them.' The crucial point is that a state which, in the name of inalienable rights, refuses to intervene in the distribution of wealth and property, is by the same token a state which neglects the poor. What the poor need is a state determined to trespass on the ground which the liberal utopia would gladly leave to the discretion of the individual; in other words, a state which is prepared to reach beyond *homo politicus*. Babeuf, indeed, epitomised practically the whole content of the ensuing century of socialist propaganda. 'It is necessary to bind together everyone's lot; to render the lot of each member of the association independent of chance, and of happy or unfavourable circumstance; to assure to every man and to his posterity, no matter how numerous it may be, as much as they need, but no more than they need.' The only means that can possibly lead to such a situation is a common administration: the political state ruled by the *demos*. What Babeuf wished to get rid of was precisely the loneliness of the isolated individual, which the bourgeois utopia eulogised and sacralised. Instead of guarding their dubious 'right to fight each other on equal terms', the state should take care of the personal and communal well-being of all individuals, so as to liberate them once and for all from the agonising uncertainty and fear of the future which competition inevitably brings about. Only such a state 'will put an end to the gnawing worm of perpetual inquietude, whether throughout society as a whole, or privately within each of us, about what tomorrow will bring, or at least what next year will bring, for our old age, for our children and for their children'. Babeuf's was the call for a welfare state, made on behalf of these who in the zero-sum game of competition expected to be the losers.

There is another idea in Babeuf's utopia which was to become a leitmotiv of socialist thought: the community should guarantee to each 'as much as they need, but no more than they need'. The idea is sometimes dismissed as a residue of the pre-industrial disbelief in the productive potential of mankind, as a sheer repetition of the defensive 'equality of poverty' in the style of More and Campanella. In fact, there is more to it; no less than an entire philosophy of human nature and its perversion. Its origin may be found in the austere scepticism of Seneca, but for Babeuf and his descendants it had probably been refurbished by Rousseau. The 'natural' needs of man are limited and one can satisfy them completely without transgressing the confines of modesty. It is not their needs which cause men to indulge in luxury and to revel in excess, but the pernicious influence of an artificially created human condition. 'The consuming ambition, the ardour to raise one's relative fortune', Rousseau wrote in his *Discourse on the Origin of Inequality among Man* (1755), 'is due less to a genuine need than to a desire to stand out from the others.' Needs are 'natural', human relations are artificial; as such they can be changed' and when changed appropriately they will remove the only motive for the human pursuit of wealth and thus return man to the 'natural' state of happiness founded on the satisfaction of his genuine needs.

The trouble with the emerging world of rampant individualism was that one could no longer derive satisfaction from the mere satisfaction of modest, unperverted needs, even if bent on resisting the splendours of affluence. A man, happy yesterday, becomes poor and so deprived today; he becomes poor 'without losing anything. Because as everything changed around him, he himself did not change at all'. For the sake of the happiness of these decent, modest men, one has to put some brakes upon change. Not necessarily in the sense of barring any further increase of the output of goods (though, not surprisingly, such an interpretation recurs time and again in the socialist literature), but in the sense of bringing some sort of constancy and stability into the network of human relations. Using a somewhat modernised terminology, one might say that a secured status would liberate man from anxieties generated by the efforts to retain it, as well as by yearnings to enhance it.

Here we come across a further and fateful departure of the socialist utopia from the liberal-bourgeois one. It was set out clearly by Saint-Amand Bazard, one of the most ardent Saint-Simonians, in his first lecture on his teacher's doctrine (delivered on 17 December 1828): what man needs more than anything else for his happiness is a 'regular social order', but such order has occurred only twice in human history – in ancient times and in the Middle Ages. The third return of the 'regular order' is still in the future. Obviously it won't be identical with the former two; but 'it will present striking analogies to them, with respect to order and unity'. Order, that is, certainty which can be furnished only by stability of the social pattern; and unity, which means freedom from the necessity to compete and to hazard one's status. Twelve years before, Robert Owen, addressing the inhabitants of his model socialist colony, stressed that permanence is the distinctive feature of that happiness which the wisely organised human community is expected to offer. Both Bazard and Owen were admittedly abstract schemers, dreaming of ready-to-wear social patterns designed in the atelier of Reason; but their concern was avowedly of an across-the-board type. Louis Auguste Blanqui, whom everybody without hesitation will place at the other end of the socialist spectrum, as the practitioner of revolutionary struggle rather than a self-appointed adviser to the Serene and the Powerful, saw precisely the 'constant uncertainty about tomorrow' as the supreme reason for a social revolution.

To sum up: the socialist utopia, in its starting-points and leit-motivs, may be justly described as 'the counter-culture of capital-ism'. The notion of a 'counter-culture' contains a dialectical and conflict-ridden unity of continuity and rejection. To be a counter-culture, a system of beliefs and postulates must engage in a signifi-cant polemic with the dominant culture, must question it, so to speak, in its own words, and to do so must speak essentially the same language in order to make the dialogue comprehensible. These conditions were fully met by the socialist utopia in relation to the dominant liberal-bourgeois utopia. It accepted in full the bourgeois ideals of the reign of justice and law, supposedly safeguarded by the institution of political equality; but it emphatically denied the pos-sibility of squaring this postulate with a free-trade economy, abandonment of the individual to his own solitude and a state which was indifferent to the anxieties of the abandoned individual. 'If you wish to enjoy political equality, abolish property', wrote Proudhon in the first chapter of his iconoclastic *What is Property?* in 1840; eight years later Louis Blanc wrote in his *Organization of Labour*: 'Freedom consists, not only in the *rights* that have been accorded, but also in the *power* given men to develop and exercise their faculties. . . . Are we for having the State intervene? . . . Most certainly. . . . Why? Because we want freedom'. To the ideal society envisaged in the ruling bourgeois utopia socialism offered a genuine alternative; but one which instead of dismissing casually the alleged virtues of the former, carried its guiding ideas much further than their original preachers intended.

It seems that the notorious convolutions of the political history of socialism were to a large extent contained already in this equivocal, dialectical relation between the bourgeois and the socialist utopias. The socialist utopia could present itself as a genuine substitute for the bourgeois way of dealing with the issues of modernity, or as a further stage into which the previous stages smoothly and imperceptibly merge.

4

The Structure of the Socialist Utopia

Having located the socialist utopia in the history of ideas, we have still to decide on the traits which define its identity, and that is admittedly a task which does not lend itself easily to an 'objective' treatment. The concept of socialism functioned in the culture of the last two centuries as a linchpin holding together a motley assortment of ideas of various degrees of specificity and elaboration. To find a community of substance which really unites them is not an easy matter. One cannot help invoking Wittgenstein's analysis of 'essences': what do all games have in common? Are they not rather objects scattered all over a broad canvas in such a way that each object shares some traits with each of its neighbours, but shares with each of them a different feature?

Having noted Wittgenstein's warning it seems well to avoid a futile attempt to extricate a common essence from all members of the historically produced family of socialist teachings, and in particular to avoid the temptation to reduce socialism as a historical phenomenon to a specific blueprint of an alternative society whose features are recognisable at first sight. Thus, it is necessary to reject from the outset many attempts of this kind which have been undertaken by a number of thoughtful scholars.

Emile Durkheim, for example, faced with the necessity of discussing socialism as a 'thing', had to be sure that he knew what sort of thing he studied. Hence the clear-cut definition: 'We denote as socialist every doctrine which demands the connection of all economic factors, or of certain among them, which are at the present time diffuse, to the directing and conscious centres of society'.[1] This notion was to be repeated, with minor modifications, by scores of scholars, both sympathetic and hostile to socialism.

Thus, Ludwig von Mises bluntly declared that socialism is 'a policy which aims at constructing a society in which the means of production are socialised. . . . I submit that one must be historically blind not to see that this and *nothing else* is what has stood for socialism for the past hundred years'.[2] And Schumpeter in his justly celebrated study wrote: 'By socialist society we shall designate an institutional pattern in which the control over means of production itself is vested with a central authority – or, as we may say, in which, as a matter of principle, the economic affairs of society belong to the public and not to the private sphere'.[3]

Apart from their determination to portray socialism as a phenomenon which stands or falls by the structure of economic relations, these and a multitude of similar definitions share another remarkable feature: their authors obviously wish to define socialism by reference to the structure of the system which socialists propose to institute, rather than the structure of socialism itself, as a body of beliefs and attitudes in its own right. They all try to answer the question: how would the world look if socialists had their way?, instead of trying to assess the role played by socialism at the moment when the socialist idea is conceived and disseminated, and its relation to the society in which it was begotten and came to be important. It is my conviction that the evident stiffness and apodictism of the definitions cited was already predetermined by the initial decision as to the universe in which the discourse of socialism is to be placed. Once this decision had been made, it seemed only natural that the right analytical frame for the study of socialism is the 'logic of blueprints' (Schumpeter), rather than logic of blueprint-need and blueprint-production.

If, however, the second logic were chosen instead of the first, the crucial question would be whether we have the right to select one specific point in socialist history as the 'maturity point', which warrants the attempt to define socialism with reference to the substance of the blueprint. One would be inclined rather to assume that the substance is doomed to remain, at any given point, inconclusive, and that it constitutes the contingent and variable element of socialism conceived as a perpetual counter-cultural alternative to the existing system. As a cultural alternative, it must be expected to react to those parameters of the social system which the current experience renders particularly obtrusive and painfully felt. One of the most important features of socialism is its intrinsic criticism of the present, inseparable from its future-orientation, which defies

all attempts to describe socialism in terms of a specific social programme given once and for all.

For this ineradicably critical spirit, socialism is again indebted
to capitalism. In Schumpeter's words, 'Capitalism creates a critical
frame of mind which, after having destroyed the moral authority
of so many other institutions, in the end turns against its own; the
bourgeois finds to his amazement that the rationalist attitude does
not stop at the credentials of kings and popes but goes on to attack
private property and the whole scheme of bourgeois values'.[4] The
bourgeois ideology started its devastating critique of absolutism
and privilege by promulgating the principle of equality in freedom
and appointing reason to the vacated office of the ultimate judge;
socialism took over the principles and accepted the appointment,
but it refused to accept that any of the social forms thus far brought
to bear can be taken as the embodiment of these principles, and
disavowed the reason incarnate in capitalist institutions as a false
messiah. The role of socialism as a constantly active critical leaven
within the texture of present society has never changed. The desire
for a just society, coupled with the renunciation of the present
one as unjust, is the most constant feature of socialism, as well
as the key to the understanding of its historical role in modern
society.

Not all criticism, of course, and not every improvement of
society, ought to be classified as a manifestation of socialism.
Socialist criticism and the socialist idea of improvement are distinguished by a specific address and a specific actual, or postulated,
sender. The socialist message is sent in the name of the deprived
and the weak, these who cannot hope to rise above the level of
destitution if they rely upon *laissez-faire* individualism. And, invariably, the message has an address as well: some kind of power,
moral or political, strong enough to curb the free-market mechanism
and compensate for the handicaps of the impoverished and the
decrepit. The content of the message, however, may vary considerably, as it did in fact when the critics of injustice began to
look beyond the implementation of the capitalist utopia of unrestrained freedom.

I have said that socialism took over from the capitalist utopia
its major ideals, and the ideal of freedom in the first place. The
capitalist utopia, however, grants freedom an undisputed top position
in its hierarchy of values, and therefore within this utopia the
familiar antinomies of freedom, though not disposed of, are reduced

to the role of minor irritants. One can argue about the freedom of others being a limitation, or a condition, of one's own freedom; one can worry about the subtle dialectical interplay between 'positive' and 'negative' freedom. In these, as in other cases of a similar kind, the antagonists, in so far as they remain on the ground of the bourgeois utopia, share the same universe of discourse and benefit from the possession of clear guidelines and unambiguous heuristic principles: it is only the demands of freedom itself which can limit freedom.

It is different in the case of the socialist utopia. Here, freedom has lost its place as the sole, supreme judge of justice; it has acquired a companion endowed with equal power, the principle of equality. Since there are now two supreme values instead of one, and since their compatibility is, to say the least, open to argument, antinomy becomes a rule; and a deadlock which can hardly satisfy either the judges or their petitioners becomes more than a contingent possibility. There is nothing in the nature of freedom as such, or in the nature of equality as such, to safeguard their consonance and prevent their conflict. The lack of cohesion and consistency within the bourgeois utopia has been repeatedly exposed, but only when the utopia itself has been submitted to criticism from an 'outside' vantage-point. More often the utopia has been used, as it should be, to criticise one or other of its supposed incarnations, on the assumption that the revealed lack of cohesion is epiphenomenal and not determined by the structure of the utopia as such. In the case of the socialist utopia, however, the proclaimed duality of supreme power condemns it, explicitly and avowedly, to a state of permanent and irremovable contradiction. The bourgeois utopia, so to speak, accords itself the benefit of the doubt and leaves it to its critics to unravel and point out its real or alleged inconsistencies, whereas it is the protagonists of the socialist utopia who have to try hard to prove that the two supreme values they expound and defend with equal vigour can be made to point unequivocally in one direction.

The intrinsic contradiction between freedom and equality became a commonsense assumption after it had been effusively discussed by Goethe and then by the great romantic poets. When Georg Simmel undertook to analyse its various aspects, he was already convinced that the existence of a problem was obvious. The shocking practice of at least one of the many 'socialist-experiments-in-action' added a new dimension to the old worry; it turned out that a skilful manipulation of the conflict-ridden wedlock may easily be abused as a cover operation for a system with a minimal, or zero, output of either freedom or equality.

The spokesmen for the above-mentioned 'experiment' dealt with the ensuing cognitive dissonance by borrowing a compromise formula, which was originally devised by the capitalist utopia in self-defence against socialist assault: the reduction of equality *in actu* to 'equality of opportunity'. It is far from clear whether 'equality of opportunity' is less antinomial than the original, boldly uncompromising, postulate. The main point is, however, that in its second, toned-down reincarnation, the ideal loses its specifically socialist flavour. 'Equality of opportunity' means, in fact, equal chances to make the best of inequality; indeed, equality of opportunity is an empty notion unless the social setting to which it refers is structured on a basis of inequality. Thus the very use of the term, in a sense, sanctifies and accepts as a constant predicament what socialism is bent on annihilating. In particular, those who use it resign themselves to the ineradicable presence of a deprived stratum and to unequal availability of the goods and benefits the system has to offer. The socialist utopia, on the contrary, is bent on elimination of specifically this kind of inequality, on compensating the deprived, on redressing inequities. So the socialist utopia is bound to face the antinomy in all its acuteness, unalleviated by sacrificing one of its inalienable postulates. This antinomy, we repeat, is the one between freedom, as the ability to realise fully one's life potential, and equality, as something true *in actu* for each and every member of the society. In this sense, the very presence of people who consider their situation as one of deprivation or oppression is subject to socialist criticism regardless of the actual or imaginary factors to which even the people in question ascribe their sufferings.

This, however, is fully compatible with the ideals of freedom and 'equality of opportunity'. Freedom to live a full and authentic life involves, among other things, freedom to rise above the level of others and to influence their behaviour, since life is always lived with and among others. An individual cannot therefore conclude that he is genuinely free if he is prevented from extending his freedom so as to impinge on the similar intentions of the others. The fuller the freedom, the greater the sacrifice of equality. Freedom seems to be, at first glance, a predicate which cannot be equally attributed to all; one which, in fact, presumes inequality, in much the same way as 'equality of opportunity' does. Freedom seems to be, indeed, the warcry of the strong in the same way as equality is the dream of the weak. The latter will regard as a realisation of equality what the first will see as an unpardonable constraint put on their freedom.

On its way from the bourgeois to the socialist utopia, therefore, the ideal of freedom underwent a subtle but significant change of meaning. Modern Socialism is, above all, the utopia of the under-dog, and this consideration colours all its constituents, including those which can be rightly viewed as the legacy of older utopias.

There was a pronounced tendency within socialist thought, though not necessarily a universal one, to reinterpret freedom as a predicate of the community rather than of the individual. In ancient Greek political thought, freedom was often understood as the ability of the *polis* to settle its own affairs without outside interference; the conflict between individual and collective freedom was not looked upon as an eternal human predicament, as it was to be much later. The conflict was largely prevented by the direct, almost un-reflective and natural participation of the individual in the *polis*. The memory of this situation returns time and again in the modern socialist utopia; socialism pretends to be about enhancing the power – the positive freedom – of the community, and *thereby* of each community member; it assumes that a really free community can afford well-nigh unlimited personal freedom of its members, and that this personal freedom afforded to everybody is a necessary condition of freedom for the community as a whole. One should remember, before dismissing this idea as a naïve paradox, that the community, as it appears in the socialist utopia, hardly ever faces the difficult problems which are widely regarded as the premise of all inequality and oppression. In particular, in the community envisaged by the socialist utopia all the goods and services people need are available in abundance. This result, so it is hoped, may be attained in two different ways: (1) the selfishness and waste which hindered the proper use of the unlimited productive capacity of society, created by capitalist industrialisation, will be removed, and through this revolutionary act alone the new socialist society will simply uncover the abundance whose potentiality has already been assured by its predecessor; or (2) socialism will eliminate the artificially swollen, superfluous needs, incited by the capitalist market, and so the same effect of relative abundance will be reached by bringing human desires and expectations back to their natural, healthy level. In the resulting conditions of abundance, the main reason for the recurring clash between individual and 'communal' interests will, it is hoped, disappear.

To be sure, the socialists sharply disagreed with each other about where one should begin constructing this harmony between the individual and his community. Split on this issue, socialists divided into two camps, more often than not engaged in a vehement struggle. From Proudhon on, one persistent current in socialist thought held to the idea of generating justice and equity 'from the bottom up', through the spontaneous, elemental activity of individuals freed from all shackles of dependency and submission. All regulation from above will tend to distort the individual's natural inclination to 'mutuality' buttressed on egalitarian justice. It seems that these socialist utopians never reached in their imagination beyond the level of the *Gemeinschaft*-like community. Construction of an integrated society on the state level from a basis of unlimited individual freedom looked, and rightly so, incredible. The vehement attacks against the government were in fact directed against a supra-communal organisation of society. That is what one might expect from critics who deplored the decline of the cosy, secure world of small farmers operating in a limited, manageable community of like-minded and like-acting people. Belief in the natural modesty of human needs, the priority given to intimate, face-to-face relations, abhorrence of supra-community government, and emphasis on freedom in the liberty-equality dyad, seem to constitute one of the two relatively cohesive syndromes within the socialist utopia.

The second camp, on the contrary, saw in the powerful machinery of the state the only lever of social justice. The power of the privileged must be crushed by an equally strong power, and the weak can acquire such power only by 'constituting themselves into a government'. Thus justice will be generated from above; equality is the premise of all genuine freedom, but equality can only be imposed upon the rich and powerful, and the state is the only means of accomplishing such a feat. This attitude, represented by thinkers otherwise so different as Karl Marx and Louis Blanc, was usually accompanied by the belief that modern technology and organisation are firmly set on integrating people on a higher societal scale, and that the process has already reached the point of no return. The wish to re-create a secure, cooperative community on this new, higher level of societal organisation completed this second syndrome.

In a sense, one may portray the difference between the two syndromes as stemming, in the last resort, from a different attitude toward capitalism and its historical role; or, in more general terms, toward the process of modernisation in its capitalist form. It is true that both currents take over the essential elements of the capitalist utopia and fill them with much more radical and explosive power; in this respect both, objectively, are located on the other side of the capitalist phase and perhaps would be impossible without this phase. Still, representatives of the two camps pronounce widely different judgements on the role played by bourgeois society in facilitating, or impeding, the advent of socialism. The first current was consistently suspicious of the way in which the spreading capitalist relations modified nearly every aspect of the society; its spokesmen denounced the irreparable harm that may be done, mostly to human motivations and moral attitudes, by the pernicious, devastating impact of submission, typical of the modern state, or of selfishness, typical of market relations. From this perspective the capitalist system looked like a perilous detour from the main track of human progress, threatening to become permanent unless reversed in time. Perhaps over-simplifying a bit, one can epitomise this view as the rule that 'The more of capitalism, the less chance for socialism'. Indeed, the current in question had no use for one achievement which undeniably could be put to the credit of capitalism; namely, the unprecedented eruption of human productive capacities and, therefore, the radical strengthening of human mastery over Nature. With this virtue of capitalism proclaimed irrelevant for a just society, envisaged as based upon 'natural' austerity, there is hardly any aspect of capitalism, apart from its remarkable flair for discrediting itself, which could be depicted as instrumental in laying the foundations of a future socialist society.

For those concerned with turning a developed society into a community-like system rather than with *preventing* the substitution of *Gesellschaft* for *Gemeinschaft*, the role of capitalism appears in a different light. For them, first of all, socialism is thinkable only as the culmination of economic progress; indeed, socialism becomes a historical possibility only because other systems, in their own cruel and ruthless way, have done the indispensable dirty job and brought human productive potential to the point of virtually complete liberation from the pressure of animal needs, thus opening the era of genuine humanity in which human life can indeed be organised according to the human principles of justice and equity. In this sense, however morally repulsive, capitalism is an essential and perhaps inevitable vehicle of the socialist future; socialism, so to speak, will take over human history at the point to which capitalism brought it before exhausting its creative potential. This idea was most emphatically expressed in the famous statement of Friedrich Engels:

> Fight on bravely then, gentlemen of capital. We need your help. We need even your rule upon occasions. For it is you who must clear from our path the relics of the Middle Ages and of absolute monarchy. You must abolish monarchy, you must centralise, you must change the more or less destitute classes into real proletarians – recruits for us. It is your factories and trade connections that must lay the foundations for the liberation of the proletariat. Your reward shall be a brief period of rule. You shall dictate laws, and bask in the sun of your own majesty. But remember, the hangman's foot is upon the threshold.

Paradoxically, both currents, though obviously each has its own distinct reasons, share the same complacent attitude toward the problems which a victorious socialist economy may encounter. The first current, committed to a simplified, 'seen-through' network of economic relations, naturally assumes that such 'problems' as may still emerge will be easily and matter-of-factly removed by means that are within everybody's reach. The second current, clearly overestimating capitalism's productive capacity and underestimating its ability to produce new needs at a faster rate than new goods, leaves it to the capitalist predecessor to render the economy unproblematic by making the dreams of abundance come true, thus reducing the task of running the economy to the venerable Saint-Simonian function of 'managing things' rather than human beings. The frequently noted 'lack of utopian blueprints', of a detailed description of the future socialist economy, in the writings of Marx was in fact a testimony to the striking consistency of his belief that capitalism will vanish from the scene taking with it into 'prehistory' not just one form of economy, but political economy as such. The putative heirs of Marx backtracked on this idea and quickly proclaimed the need of a political economy of socialism; but this was not the socialism Marx foresaw.

As we have already observed, because of the preoccupation of Marxism, by far the most influential form of socialism, with the economic system as the foundation of social power, it has become customary to identify the socialist utopia above all with a vision of a radically remodelled economy. The error consists in the reversal of priorities. All currents of socialist thought in fact agreed that the economy is important, in the first place, as an immense enslaving power, barring men from developing their full human potentialities. The economy is, therefore, a hurdle to be removed, an encumbrance to be rendered harmless. This could be achieved, socialists agreed again, by the simultaneous accomplishment of two complementary tasks: (1) Quantitatively a balance of production and needs must be achieved by either raising the first or lowering the second, and in this way freedom from want must be secured. All human freedom starts from this basis, and without it no freedom is thinkable, much less attainable; but freedom from want is only a first step on the road, on which man can face and come to grips with the really important and more sophisticated dilemmas of his condition. (2) Qualitatively economic considerations must be prevented from playing the pernicious role of a major motive of human behaviour, fomenting greed, envy, mutual suspiciousness and hatred, and prodding people endlessly to pursue material gain with little or no relation to the degree in which their economic needs have been satisfied.

With the economy in these two virulent roles out of the way, man will finally be able to grapple with the major issues of his emancipation. It is only natural that in so far as the most brutal and poignant material needs dominate man's concerns and cast their shadow on his whole perception of the world, the solution of economic problems may become not simply a major obstacle, but a final goal of human liberation, thereby developing from a subsidiary and instrumental to a consummatory role. It may seem that with the solution of the economic problem everything else will automatically follow. In fact, as Henry Smith rightly remarked, this solution means at best the elimination of 'an intolerable nuisance'; a precondition, but hardly a determinant, of the 'ultimate freeing of the human spirit',[5] the end which – even if temporarily pushed into the background – loomed large as the ultimate ideal of the socialist utopia. An uncurbed and untarnished human happiness was the dream shared with the bourgeois utopia; but what the bourgeois utopia could offer only to the strong and successful, the socialist one wished to give to all, and to the underdog above all. That was the most important reason why it could not accept the network of economic relations bequeathed by capitalism. As a motto to his *Garantien der Harmonie und Freiheit* (1842), Wilhelm Weitling wrote: 'We want to be as free as the birds of the air; we want to go through life in joyful bands, just as they do, with never a thought of care'. In Fourier's commune of the future, work would become a pleasant pastime. For Marx, socialist man would perform various jobs useful for the community in a relaxed, happy manner, simply releasing his intrinsic drive for creativity, as an autotelic rather than instrumental activity. Lafargue wrote a treatise on the human 'right to laziness', while Jaures called his doctoral dissertation 'un hymne de bonheur'. Karl Korsch brought the ultimate goal of the socialist utopia into a sharper relief than most other writers: 'From the very first day, this genuine proletarian dictatorship will be distinguished from every false imitation of it by its creation of the conditions of intellectual freedom not only for "all" workers but for "each individual" worker. . . . Socialism, both in its ends and in its means, is a struggle to realise freedom'.[6]

From the outset this thrust for freedom comes into sharp conflict with the community orientation, so essential for a utopia bent upon the defence of the deprived and the weak. It is difficult to challenge the penetrating insight of Gustav Le Bon, none the less topical for being nearly a century old: 'What in effect is Socialism, speaking philosophically: or, at least, what is its best-known form, Collectivism? Simply a reaction of the collective being against the encroachment of the individual being. . . . Only the strong can support isolation, and rely only on themselves; the weak are unable to do so'.[7] Le Bon shows the intimate link between championship of the cause of the weak and readiness to propound the superiority of the collectivity over the individual. As was pointed out earlier, the conciliation between freedom and security of the weak, freedom and the prevention of deprivation, has been, still is, and certainly will remain the focal antinomy of the socialist utopia. This is clearly seen by sympathisers as well as by adversaries of socialism, whose attitude was ably epitomised by Lord Acton; he deplored the 'throwing away' of 'the finest opportunity ever given to the world . . . because the passion for equality made vain the hope for freedom'. Remodelling economic life no longer seems to be an important enough event to reconcile the eternal enemies; nor does a specific form of ownership bear the responsibility for this enmity.

Having lost its faith in solving the conflict *en route*, while getting the injustice-generating economic institutions out of the way, the socialist utopia is doomed to live with the antinomy and its consequences.

The major consequence is an irreducible diversity of attitudes which claim to be accommodated under the socialist umbrella. A measure of trade-off being unavoidable in each case, the focus of attention and priority may shift over a wide range of values from a virtually unlimited freedom of the individual to the unrestrained sway of the community over 'private interests'. In both cases the attitude taken is, of course, highly critical of the deficiencies of capitalism, but the critique is aimed at different aspects of the system. From Proudhon on, the champions of freedom have assailed the capitalist system mainly for its failure to deliver on its pledge to liberate the individual from all and any constraint placed on him by a superior authority; capitalist freedom is a sham, they would say, and would not become real unless the stolen means of production and influence were redeemed. From Fourier on, the preachers of communal authority and control have exposed the sell-out of the interests of the multitude for the sake of the freedom of the few, and advocated the redress of this injustice as a supreme goal, whose attainment may require a suppression of individual freedom. When extrapolated from these two extreme standpoints, the proposals of the socialist utopia may point to ends as widely divergent as an anarchic, ungoverned collectivity and a radical, dictatorial concentration of power and control in the hands of societal agencies. This is, therefore, the second issue which splits the socialist camp right down the middle; and like the previous one, it has its ultimate source in the immanent antinomy of the values socialism is committed to pursuing. This division overlaps only partially with the first. One would expect the anarchistic tendencies not to reach beyond the community level; but they are far from having an exclusive concern with this level. And among the socialists who focus attention upon the greater society rather than the *Gemeinschaft*-like community, the division is just as pronounced and conflict-generating.

The third antinomy is between history as a lawful process, and creative action. It was contained already in the – originally Kantian – double-pronged concept of law inherited and fully adopted by the socialist utopia. In his review of Herder's *Ideen zur Philosophie der Geschichte der Menschheit*, Kant formulated the idea, later to be turned into a major pivot of the Hegelian system, that the destiny of the human race *is* to move consistently toward a crowning idea, and that, according 'to the plan of Providence', men *have to* direct their exertions to this end. The statement is inherently ambiguous; progress is, so to speak, 'predetermined' and its direction is pre-ordained; but its 'predetermination' consists solely in men having to pursue it and eventually bring it to pass. The law of history, there-fore, has a double sense: that of a 'natural necessity' and that of a norm of human behaviour. The idea appears again, on a much grander scale, in Hegel. The Spirit envelops history through the actions of nations; nations are immanent in the historical process but unfree; the Spirit is free, but transcendent. It is enough to substitute the informed consciousness, founded (according to nine-teenth-century standards) on scientific analysis, for the metaphysical Spirit, and oppressed classes for nations, to move into the very midst of the third dilemma of the socialist utopia.

In *Socialism, Utopian and Scientific*, probably the best-known of his works, Engels wrote the famous and often recalled passage:

Active social forces work exactly like natural forces: blindly, forcibly, destructively, so long as we do not understand, and reckon with, them. But when once we understand them, when once we grasp their action, their direction, their effects, it depends only upon ourselves to subject them more and more to our own will, and by means of them to reach our own ends.

Thus far Engels's words sound like a mundane positivist profes-sion of faith, which Comte would eagerly have countersigned. But if seen against the background of Marx's dialectics of history and action, the statement acquires a new dimension. Men are not free to choose when they are willing to 'understand' the 'active social forces'; moreover, their eventual understanding depends on much more than just a right methodology and diligent study. Some men are doomed to false consciousness with no hope of liberation. It is history itself, acting blindly and forcibly, which leads at some point to a situation in which the relative universality turns into an absolute and final one, and therefore the knowledge of reality may become clear and true in both time directions. Mankind then enters the unique situation in which the historical predicament of man may be sensed and described in its real character as historical, instead of being expressed in a myth which portrays history as nature (thereby suggesting the inevitable and conclusive character of historically transient phenomena and denying the creative ability of human action).

According to the Marxist doctrine this unique situation has arrived now for the first time in human history. The means of production – whose private appropriation was throughout history the major source of oppression, particularism of class interests and hence false consciousness – have now reached truly 'social' proportions and begun to explode the narrow framework of private ownership. If they have not exploded it yet, that is because the class which rests its domination on this basis defends it actively and effectively; but when the resistance is finally broken the system which emerges will be the first in which human universality will not be mediated and distorted by the class membership of the individual. Hence, the universal platform from which criticism of the existing form of class oppression is launched is the first in history which will remain universal even when its critical task is accomplished and the present ruling class is toppled. And so, again for the first time in history, a complete and unreserved identity of conscious human action and history may be achieved; by simplifying and rendering transparent the network of human conflicts, the previously blind and elemental nature-like history has reached a stage at which its rules may be known in full and therefore its later development may be entirely conscious and cut to the measure of universal human welfare.

This idea of a 'historically determined freedom from history' occurred to Marx relatively early, in the process of rethinking the legacy of Hegel. The idea indeed retained, until translated much later into the language of political economy, its distinctly Hegelian wrappings, evident in the terminology as clearly as in the substance. In somewhat less philosophical form, purified of the mediating role of consciousness as a reflection of the transparency of social relations, the idea of the new era as a unique juncture of history and conscious human action remained in the forefront of the socialist utopia. The shape it usually took may be well illustrated by one example, taken from the notorious Ferdinand Lassalle's *Working Class Programme* (1862):

It is this opposition, gentlemen, between personal interest and the development of the nation in culture, which the lower classes, happily for them, are without. . . . You are in the happy position that the idea which constitutes your true personal interest is one with the throbbing pulse of history, and with the living principle of moral development. You are able therefore to devote yourselves with personal passion to this historical development.

In another version of the same idea, Georg Lukács would say three-quarters of a century later that each class imposes on the society an artificial order of its own making, but presents it as nature; the proletariat will be no exception so far as the artificiality of its order is concerned, but it will be able to say it openly, since its artificiality is very much in line with the universal interests of men.

In one form or another the idea that the most deprived and oppressed parts of society are the carriers of historical progress seems to be essential to socialist thought in all its many variations. But one can interpret in many ways, sharply distinct in their practical consequences, the paradigm of the history-and-action mix. There is some evidence for the view that one of the important reasons that led German social democracy, after much hesitation, to embrace the Marxist conception of the transition to socialism was that with due emphasis on 'historical inevitability' one need have no compunction about pursuing a policy only tenuously related to the end it was supposed to serve. Indeed, one can satisfy oneself in this way that history will – somehow, some time – 'see to it' that capitalism will collapse and that socialism will triumph; or, on the contrary, in a Calvinistic mood, one can reject quietism precisely as an unhistorical attitude and try to speed up the vacillating process by direct and determined action, suspecting perhaps that history has no other vehicle by which to impose its laws on the human condition. The tension between these two attitudes, equally legitimate in the light of the central idiom and equally 'undetermined' by it, constituted the paramount feature of the Marxist theoretical system and expressed itself in the immanent contradiction – as Gianfranco Poggi recently put it – between the assumption of the essential open-endedness of the human situation and an overwhelming tendency to 'empirically close' it by unveiling its historical determinants. On the whole, the antinomy of history versus action seemed to be largely independent of the other two, those of state versus community and of freedom versus equality. With the former two divisions only partly overlapping, one can perhaps accept these three axes as the three dimensions designating the space of the socialist utopia, as well as its structure, its major dilemmas and its tensions.

5

Utopia and Commonsense

The last dilemma is however closer than the other two to the practical task of achieving socialism; it is located, so to speak, right on the bridge connecting the utopia of today with the reality of tomorrow. The vexing dilemma which each and every socialist utopia-in-action is bound to face is this: socialism means a radical departure from present conditions, but it can be accomplished only if a proper account is taken of these conditions. Moreover, it must be set in motion by factors which have already been gestated and developed within these conditions. The socialist project is therefore caught between a suicidal adventurism on one side and a no less suicidal compromise with 'realism' on the other. The fact is that a well-established social structure does not, on the whole, facilitate major revolutionary departures from the existing order; it has, by and large, an in-built mechanism of self-perpetuation.

These mechanisms have been described variously, but with a great measure of accord, by the dominant, functionalist-influenced brand of sociology as well as by the most thoughtful Marxist theoreticians. By far the most perspicacious, however, seems to be Antonio Gramsci's model of the 'historical bloc', as the match between a particular social structure, seen above all as the network of economic dependencies, and the cultural and political 'superstructure'. Gramsci ascribes the vital role in sustaining the historical bloc to 'civil society', which he, in an apparent opposition to Marx's elaboration of this Hegelian term, regards as a vital constituent of the superstructure rather than the structure itself. According to Gramsci, civil society comprises the sphere of ideology and is operated mostly by intellectuals; it sustains the conditions of a specific class rule and the everyday, habitual behaviour of the bulk of the society, by securing their reciprocal sustaining and reinvigoration. Civil society may be seen as the cultural hegemony of a specific social group over the totality of the society; or as the ethical content of a class-dominated state.

Ideology, or the ruling cultural idiom of the society, supplies the total world-view which directly or indirectly regulates human conduct, rendering it orderly, rule-governed and predictable. This cultural idiom is, to be sure, arranged in a hierarchy of varying degrees of specificity, sophistication, and explicit ideological involvement. At the top there is philosophy, which in each particular period is split into currents engaged in an allegedly mortal struggle, but which can be seen, from the proper perspective, as unified to the extent of assuring its own functionality toward a particular historical bloc; this unity is attained by the sharing of an essential set of 'Weltanschauung' premises. Provided the latter condition is met, the very functionality of philosophy hinges precisely on its heterogeneity, which facilitiates the accommodation of a variety of interests, articulated to a varying extent, within the historical bloc in question. At the bottom there is commonsense, or the 'folklore of philosophy'. It expresses itself in everyday social and economic behaviour, in the attitudes spontaneously, unreflectively, naïvely assumed toward those problems and situations with which the 'orderly' functioning society may confront its members. Such commonsense is seldom articulated directly; if it is, it takes the form of an 'economic-corporative' consciousness which is inevitably 'inorganic' in the sense of not being able to generate, much less sustain, a new cultural idiom which would be likely to dissolve the existing civil society and construct a new one. In an alienated society, that is, in a society in which the means of control are located beyond the reach of individual members of the oppressed groups, inarticulate commonsense demands an obedient acceptance of the imposed range of options and limits of manoeuvre, as well as verbalising life-tasks and ambitions in matching terms; the 'economic-corporative', imperfect articulation of commonsense will involve transcending the individual's range of options, but only as a purely quantitative multiplication of individual potentialities, still confined squarely to the locus assigned to the group in question within the historical bloc. The inorganic nature of the purely trade-union kind of economic-corporative articulation consists, for example, in the fact that far from shattering the principle of market bargaining, it reasserts and strengthens its sway over group commonsense.

In a fully developed capitalist society, according to Gramsci, the ruling group maintains its supremacy by intellectual and moral leadership rather than by coercion or the blatant suppression of resistance. Gramsci hotly contested the Bolshevik-inspired tendency to 'statelatry', to playing up the role of the political state in a double sense: first, as the most powerful pillar of capitalist rule; second, as the major end of a socialist insurrection, whose capture allegedly establishes socialist rule. If the bourgeoisie achieves a real hegemony, in terms of intellectual and moral leadership based on the dominant cultural idiom which effectively permeates the commonsense level, the state, with its coercive powers and specialised organs of suppression, is relegated to the role of an advanced trench. Its capture leaves the really elaborate and powerful system of defences virtually intact. With civil society unaffected, one can only expect that in the wake of a purely political battle civil society will gain ascendency over the state rather than the other way round.

It is true that Gramsci was somewhat more tolerant about the error of 'statelatry' in the case of the situation confronted by the Bolsheviks themselves in Russia. In the tsarist-ruled society, civil society was virtually non-existent. Instead of exercising hegemony, tsarist rule was founded on naked domination; the political state was engaged directly in the continual suppression of the nation. One can say that the state relied directly on the suppressed, debased, and submissive commonsense of the inarticulate multitude, with only a jelly-like intellectual stratum in between. In these circumstances, the capture of state power could indeed become a decisive factor in the socialist upheaval, provided that this state was utilised immediately as a major leverage for a real civil society, meant to sustain the socialist historical bloc, by creating and securing the supremacy of a new, socialist, cultural idiom. No such development is thinkable, however, in the case of Western societies, thoroughly processed by the long history of capitalist institutions, in which the rule of the bourgeoisie is one of hegemony rather than of domination.

Here, civil society is the decisive battlefield between capitalism and socialism. The strategic aim of the struggle is the replacement of the bourgeois by the socialist cultural idiom; its tactical goal is to establish a strong link between a part of the intellectuals and the subordinate classes, as well as to halt the progress of 'transformism', the slow but steady 'decapitation' of the subordinate classes through co-optation of the successive echelons of their intellectual elites. In the conditions of a mature capitalist society, in which the leadership of the bourgeoisie has an intellectual and moral nature, socialism can establish itself only as a new cultural idiom which remoulds commonsense. The road toward destruction of the capitalist 'historical bloc' leads through the disintegration of its civil society, in the main by developing a new culture within the old structure.

It will be seen immediately that the battle for commonsense is replete with dangerous traps. Capitalism, like any established system, has a powerful edge over any of its potential adversaries in that its very reality, the structure of the everyday situations which it creates for the individual, reaffirms and reinforces the capitalism-sustaining brand of commonsense even without an open intervention of refined intellectual arguments. It lends the habitual patterns of conduct a spurious air of naturalness and eternity; and it stamps everyday routine as rational behaviour, having previously established the value of rationality as a supreme criterion of worthiness. Moreover, the ruling class can rely on the fact that its culture, once established, defines all imaginable improvement as an advance in acquisition of this very culture. Even a powerful thrust toward amelioration, therefore, can hardly fracture the cultural foundation of the current hegemony; if anything, it will rather reinforce it by adding a new strength and popularity to its constituent value-patterns.

It is clear that Gramsci accords to the intellectuals a substantially more important role than either orthodox Marxism or the labour-oriented brands of socialism would be willing to grant. In Gramsci's model intellectuals occupy the strategically central place, for the simple reason that the struggle for socialism is above all the struggle for a new culture. One need not agree entirely with Gramsci's emphasis on the cultural essence of socialism in order to accept his argument that culture is indeed the field of the most decisive battle, since socialism cannot make a real advance so long as the dominant commonsense is cut to the measure of the capitalist system. At some point commonsense must undergo a drastic change if utopia is even to approach the stage of becoming a reality. Otherwise one would perhaps find insightful the caustic remark of Le Bon, that the realisation of the basic tenets of the socialist utopia 'will clash fatally with the economic and psychological necessities. . . . And therefore the hour of the advent of Socialism will undoubtedly be the hour of its decline'.[1]

The fear that the deprived and the oppressed have of liberating themselves, or, indeed, of lending their unreserved support to the effort of liberation, has incessantly haunted the socialist ranks, and particularly their more radical and uncompromising sectors. Watching the practice of his socialist contemporaries, Werner Sombart thought it possible even to define socialism as attempts 'to show the proletariat the goal of its efforts, to call upon it to take up the struggle, to organise the struggle, to show it the way along which it must march if it is to succeed'.[2] Sombart's words faithfully reflected the view widely held by expanding social democracy, as epitomised in Kautsky's definition of the party as the 'confluence of socialism and the working class'. In keeping with the dominant cultural idiom, the respectability of the socialist idea was seen in its resulting from a careful and disciplined scientific analysis; but science is the work of intellectuals and, by definition, not of the proletariat. Therefore, although it draws its ultimate reason from the deplorable condition of the oppressed, it can come to them only from outside. As Kautsky wrote, in the paragraph enthusiastically endorsed by Lenin in *What Is To Be Done?*

> Socialist consciousness is represented as a necessary and direct result of the proletarian class struggle. But this is absolutely untrue. Of course, Socialism, as a theory, has its roots in modern economic relationships in the same way as the latter emerges from the struggle against the capitalist-created poverty and misery of the masses. But Socialism and the class struggle arise side by side and not one out of the other; each arises out of different premises. Modern socialist consciousness can arise only on the basis of profound scientific knowledge. . . . The vehicles of science are not the proletariat, but the bourgeois intelligentsia. It was out of the hearts of members of this stratum that modern Socialism originated. . . . Thus Socialist consciousness is something introduced into the proletarian struggle from without, and not something which arose within it spontaneously.

The workers, so to speak, must be *taught*, and their teachers are intellectuals. All the emphasis, in practice if not in theory, is on the other side of the dyad, since the spontaneously developing class struggle is organically incapable of developing into a struggle for socialism; indeed, the two arise 'out of different premises'.

But what could the intellectuals offer the workers? In his remarkably insightful analysis of the practice of German social democracy Gunther Roth showed that the offer in fact boiled down to the noble idea of elevating the uneducated, 'uncultured' worker to the highest levels of *Kultur*, of transforming him into a genuine, refined *Kulturmensch*, by an assiduous effort in his physical, intellectual and political *Bildung*.[3] In Gramscian terms, that would be precisely what civil society, and the intellectuals as its major vehicle, are expected to accomplish in the way of securing the hegemony of the present ruling class, of linking the dominant philosophy with commonsense. Roth showed admiringly how the idea and the ensuing practice led to the emergence of a vast, highly institutionalised subculture within the dominant culture of Imperial Germany, and, in effect, to the relatively smooth incorporation of workers into modern society all apparent friction notwithstanding. Bebel was right, though probably not in the sense he intended, when he described social democracy as 'the leaven which forces bourgeois society ahead'. The subculture with its elaborate institutions – its own press, literature, schools, social clubs, rest homes etc. – catered for the most variegated needs of the working population which were left unsatisfied by the institutions of the greater society, but it satisfied them in full accordance with the dominant cultural idiom. Indeed, social democracy increasingly discouraged the illusion, held by some of its intellectual sympathisers, that the social revolution of socialism should be coupled with and spearheaded by an equally daring cultural experiment; and it tried hard, with total success, to prune its cultural message of all side-shoots considered 'uncultured' by the standards of the dominant ideal. The pattern seems to repeat itself again and again, in social democracy first and then in the powerful and well-entrenched communist parties; the struggle to conquer civil society results more often than not in the quiet and peaceful, hardly noticeable process of assimilation of the originally insurgent intellectuals. Civil society reasserts itself, now richer and more inclusive than before, having incorporated the potentially disruptive elements; indeed, the phenomenon of 'transformism' occurs again. Far from having defeated the bourgeois-inspired commonsense, the intellectuals, it seems, have succeeded in dissolving in it the originally intransigent socialist utopia, in 'taming' socialism, blunting its cutting edge, transforming the very term into a household word used to describe a limited, 'economic-corporative' interest.

At the other pole, we find the view that education, however intense and well-organised, cannot, in so far as it takes place within bourgeois society, bridge the gap between socialism and the working class. The holders of this view agreed with their adversaries that there is nothing intrinsically socialist in the everyday proletarian struggle for a partial improvement of the terms of exchange; but they refused to believe that one can impregnate this struggle with more socialism inside capitalist society, when the everyday routine fosters and fortifies the 'corruption' (Babeuf) of the masses and their 'commonsensical' submission to the existing order. The passage to socialism may occur only in a 'flash', as a result of a shock violently disrupting the monotonous routine of everyday life. It may happen in the liberating, spontaneous experience of a general strike (Sorel), when the workers suddenly discover their power thus far concealed behind scattered and isolated manifestations of their 'economic-corporative' interests. Again, it may happen thanks to the lonely individual 'martyrs' (Lavrov) who will loom high over the 'mob' as an uncanny, unattainable ideal, but who will 'inspire thousands with the energy they need for their struggle'. Or, it may happen if capitalism is forced to abandon all appearances and embark on a naked, undisguised and ruthless violence thus forcing the masses into the necessity of a final and unambiguous choice. A common denominator for all these views is the conviction that the oppressed classes, the real carriers of the socialist-utopia-in-action, cannot be 'educated to socialism' in an anti-socialist society; their real education can begin only after the change of political rule. The new socialist culture will be generated by a new political power rather than the other way round. Hence the idea of a transitional period, broached constantly by the revolutionary wing; the important point is that this period must begin, not end, with the change of political power. Since, by definition, the workers are not mature enough to embrace socialism the moment power changes hands, the power throughout the transitional period will not be exercised by the workers themselves. The body politic after the political revolution will wield domination over the not-yet-socialist masses in the name of the implementation of the socialist idiom. The question is, of course, whether this form of domination will be more conducive to the socialist culture taking root than are other forms of political domination.

This contradiction between the utopian thrust and the recalcitrant 'actuality' institutionalising and effectively protecting the former *telos*, should be seen as the most embarrassing antinomy of all those which have haunted modern socialism up to the present time. This is an antinomy which socialism shares with all other utopias and, indeed, all other counter-cultures; it pertains to the general question of how the implementation of utopia is possible at all, in so far as utopia, by definition, means a radical intellectual departure from the existing dominant culture.

The gravity of the problem, though certainly immense, has been hyperbolised by the way in which the antinomy has been posited, accepting the absolute nature of the contradiction between thought and actuality, brought into focus by the historical process of alienation. It takes as its starting-point, in other words, the duality of man as a creature determined by his social reality and determining only his own thought. Given the alienation of the means of control, man as a subject is a lonely and helpless creature, confined to his private thinking. Thought is therefore disarmed in the face of reality. The two, moreover, are mutually impenetrable. 'The social reality' exists independently of what people think, and is not likely to be changed by the introduction and dissemination of new ideas. Unless a 'third force' is used (e.g. political power) critical thought and the criticised reality will perhaps coexist, with time remaining on the side of reality, as the 'hard' partner in the game.

The search for a 'third force' has indeed constituted the better part of the history of socialism, at least of those currents which keeping a wary eye on the 'magic 51 per cent' formula, foresee an inescapable dilution of the socialist end in the impure concoction of parliamentary means. Even if they avoided venting their misgivings in public, most socialists did not believe that the counter-culture of socialism would assert itself in the hostile environment of capitalist reality. The view fairly commonly shared was that only a violent shock can bring forth the desired 'rupture' in habitual behaviour. The anarchist wing was probably the most hopeful of all; its thinkers assumed that the 'tough' kernel of reality which keeps the masses at bay and prevents their creative self-realisation is the political violence of the state. Remove the state, and the long-contained energy of the people will explode, shaping freely the contours of the new, unfettered and just society. Therefore, it is not too important which force will eventually do the job of toppling the state. Bakunin, for example, attached much hope to the 'unleashing of brutal passions', and thought that such dramatic conduct is most likely in the case of the most desperate men, whose situation is intimidating beyond endurance, and who have no stake to lose whatever course their struggle takes. Such men are to be found among young *déclassé* bourgeois, or among the impoverished, brutalised eastern European peasants, or among the modern brands of the Roman-type proletariat, well represented by the *lazzaroni* of Naples. Since the opening of the socialist era begins and ends with the destruction of the state, these people, acting as a vanguard, may be seen as the truly revolutionary force. Even if they fail to reach their strategic aim, they will still score an important tactical success; they will expose the vulnerability and 'this-worldliness' of the allegedly invincible and sacred, and thereby shock the masses out of their habitual resigned docility. In this sense, no revolution is entirely lost, however discouraging its short-term consequences may be; there is a cleansing, liberating quality in each revolt, in every refusal to obey. Tkachev was even more explicit on this point than Lavrov: 'If they see that the terrible power before which they used to tremble and abase themselves is disorganised, disunited, helpless, defiled and they do not need to be afraid of anybody or anything, then the repressed feeling of bitterness and the demand for revenge will break out with irresistible force.'

While the anarchists hoped mostly for a 'demonstration effect' of open revolt committed by a fearless and determined minority, other socialists, in their search for the emancipating 'rupture', looked for a massive explosion of popular indignation, which the blending of socialist propaganda with the unbearable sufferings of the oppressed would eventually bring into effect. This was the idea of the general strike, an event totally distinct from the anarchist revolt in that it involved, right from the start, an active and enthusiastic participation of the broadest masses. The liberating quality of a general strike consists neither in destroying the state power which supposedly is the only obstacle to freedom 'here and now', nor in heartening the scared masses by a dramatic example, but in the direct involvement of the masses in the active historical process, in the immediate exercise of this 'transcendence' of the subject-object split which is the nub of the socialist emancipation from alienation of power and control. The general strike seemed to be an act of just such transcendence, overcoming, in one fell swoop, the allegedly inescapable disjunction between thought and actuality; the massive, history-creating action seemed to be a perfect blend of the two supposedly non-communicating adversaries. That is why so many prominent socialists, otherwise so distinct from each other, from Rosa Luxemburg to Edward Bernstein, from Kurt Eisner to Aristide Briand, looked to the general strike as a final and irrevocable marriage between socialism and the oppressed masses.

c*

The importance of the general strike, as a specimen of the class of direct action, was that the masses acted against the rules of capitalist society; in practice, and not just in their private thoughts, they transgressed the boundaries of bourgeois commonsense. This experience of 'looking beyond', and by the same token of bringing this 'beyond' out, is conspicuously lacking in the piecemeal 'reformist' pursuits of the socialist-inspired politicians. For this reason Rosa Luxemburg thought that social reforms, far from assaulting capitalist property and interfering with capitalist exploitation, in fact protect both, lending them order and regularity. This view was commonly interpreted as an expression of a 'the worse, the better' attitude, or the assumption that social reforms are harmful for the socialist cause because they render labour conditions less intolerable, and workers less prone to dissent. In fact, Rosa Luxemburg was repelled by the 'from above' nature of social reforms, by the fact that they are accomplished in an orderly fashion as defined by the capitalist state, with little or no involvement of the workers themselves, with the workers remaining immobilised in their position of objects of action, of recipients, of the 'acted upon'. In this more subtle, though none the less dangerous way, social reforms reinforce the kind of commonsense which sustains bourgeois hegemony. The fact that as a result of the reforms some enterprises will change hands, pass from private owners to hired managers, will not in the least affect the subordinate status of the masses as objects rather than subjects of history, and certainly will not lift them to the level of a new hegemonic class. The same reservation applies in full to the trade-union struggle. While it involves a more active attitude on the part of the workers it still stops short of transcending the boundary lines of the bargaining process. Only a general strike, smashing the fences which divide economic-corporative groups from each other, can accomplish the miracle of emancipation from yesterday's commonsense and thus open the way to a new historical bloc. This emancipation will not be attained through 'empiricism' and 'realism', the two pragmatic principles which stand for submission to commonsense, and through it to the current model of hegemony.

One can say that the attempts to solve the antinomy now under discussion led many a socialist thinker to a conclusion, not always explicit, that the passage to socialism will require socialist means; that not all kinds of action, regardless of their apparently 'socialist' consequences, bring a new socialist historical bloc any closer. This assumption makes sense in so far as one understands socialism as a totally novel culture, with a new dominant philosophy, a new concept of reality and of human potentialities, new ways of incorporating the individual biography into societal history, and new patterns of interhuman relations, rather than as a mere institutional change in the titles of ownership or a reshuffling of the ruling garrison. This was, it seems, the way Marx understood socialism. Only if this is true can one comprehend why Marx insisted that no historical system would vanish unless it exhausted its creative potential, and that socialism will therefore crown a long epoch of capitalist development; and why he found it so difficult to answer recurrent Russian questions concerning the possibility of a 'short-cut' way from the peasant community to socialism; and why he looked so intently toward all manifestations of spontaneous, massive revolutionary action, rather than toward the parliamentary activities of professional politicians.

Considering the historical tendencies of capitalist accumulation, Marx foresaw two parallel processes: on the one hand, the huge development of technological mastery over Nature, which was likely to end natural scarcity; on the other hand, the radical polarisation of power and wealth which would make the situation of the proletariat intolerable. These two tendencies were, according to Marx, closely interconnected. The abolition of the capitalist system will become 'inevitable' only when the means of production develop to their utmost capacity within capitalism. Marx did not regard socialism as a system that competed with capitalism in managing the economy 'more efficiently'. It hardly occurred to Marx that 'socialism' might be confronted with the task of developing the productive potential and fighting scarcity; the historical mission of creating the conditions of universal wealth and opulence was to be accomplished within the framework of bourgeois rule. Socialism was seen, therefore, as an act of revendication of power and control that was already there, though expropriated and alienated; and the nub of the socialist revolution, far from being limited to an economic or proprietary reform, consisted in restoring to the expropriated the role of conscious and free subjects of history. It seems that Marx linked this act of restitution to the final phase of capitalist accumulation because he did not believe that historical freedom was feasible unless men shook off the limitation imposed on them by still untamed Nature. Capitalism, so Marx hoped, would tame Nature; socialism would transform society from a natural-like, blind and intractable 'over there', into a conscious process of historical creativity.

To put it briefly, Marxist socialism was not about the management of the economy, and not even about the forms of ownership, but about the activity of the masses. This essence of Marxist socialism, which has since been lost in the bureaucratised, administered practice of Western socialism and communism – so it can be argued – was grasped by Lenin and his associates; but only to be applied in conditions to which, according to Marx, it was utterly inapplicable.

6

A Socialist Experiment

It hardly occurred to Marx that socialism would arrive before capitalism had 'exhausted' its creative potential, and he believed that this potential was sufficient to raise the productive forces of the society to the level of abundance. In this perspective, socialism could be located squarely in the political and cultural sphere of the social organisation; it would be possible, indeed, only in so far as the capitalist venture, in its own crude and ruthless manner, liberated society from economic scarcity and, therefore, from slavery to Nature and necessity.

The Marxist idiom, however, was taken over and used as a revolutionary call to arms in countries which hardly fit the Marxist description of a society 'ripe' for socialism. The peasantry has been invited to carry out the Marxist revolution; the same peasantry whose disappearance Marx counted among the main conditions for anybody to enter the kingdom of socialist reason.

In consequence, the Marxist leaders of the peasant revolution were confronted, the day after they had captured state power, with a number of vital questions which had never been considered by Marx in the context of the socialist system and were obviously incompatible with the Marxian notion of socialism as the final act of human liberation.

'One of the central preoccupations of the Bolshevik leaders', wrote Alex Inkeles in his somewhat belated, but scathing and pointed criticism of the one-sidedly 'totalitarian' models of the Soviet system, 'was to organise things so that they really ran'.[1] Sure enough, any revolutionary power faces the same encumbrance, for the twin reason of its own incompetence and inexperience in 'getting things done' and the general turmoil and breach of routine which afflicts the society 'on the morning after' the revolution. But the ordinary discomforts of a victorious revolution were magnified in the case of the Bolsheviks by the sheer grandiosity of their ambitions. In a somewhat perverted form the peculiarity of their problems was repeatedly harped on by Stalin: the bourgeois revolution needs only to remove the political obstacles which curb the already mature productive forces and relations; the Soviet revolution, on the contrary, had to use political power to build the new forces and relations from scratch.

One cannot be sure whether the leaders of the revolution saw their task from the start in the way it was to be formulated later, in retrospect, by Stalin. There are many signs to suggest that at the beginning they tended to contain the task of the socialist revolution in the sphere of social and political reforms, hoping perhaps that the flourishing of human productivity would somehow follow, thus disposing, in the process, of all awkward economic questions. As late as 1921 the Soviet leaders were still bent on revolutionising directly and immediately the productive relations rather than the productive forces, and thus, so to speak, reaching for socialism while side-stepping the long and tortuous process of forging the modern means of production together with the workmanship required to set them in motion. The 'war communism' period could only partly be interpreted as an extemporaneous response to the vicissitudes of the civil war; it was understood at least as much by its champions as a gradual approximation to the socialist utopia in a direct, short-cut way. Workers' control over all facets of factory activity was encouraged and thought of as a 'matter-of-course' development, the upper limit of the administrators' income was implacably observed, and the equality of consumption was considered anything but a temporary measure to be dropped when better times arrived. During 1920 and 1921 a number of decrees declared free distribution of important goods, and on the very eve of NEP the government agencies were working on another decree abolishing all taxation, as an introductory step to a gradual elimination of currency and money exchange. By that time, the annual production reached the all-time low of 9.4 per cent of that of 1913.

The sudden volte-face to NEP found many people psychologically and ideologically unprepared, and however obvious its reasons it encountered strong and resolute resistance in many communist circles. It took all the enormous authority of Lenin to impose the new policy against the will of numerous leaders steeped in the traditional image of socialism as mainly a social and moral revolution. The reluctance to accept Lenin's argument can be attributed to the revulsion most Marxists must have felt at the thought of admitting the capitalist, only just chased away, back into Soviet life. But in no less a measure it may be ascribed to a total upheaval in the way the task of Soviet power was to be understood, which the idea of NEP implied. Not only did Lenin suggest that the admission of private capital may be the most expedient and painless way to economic reconstruction; he put the task of developing the economy for the first time clearly and unambiguously at the top of the Bolshevik priorities. He exhorted the revolutionaries of yesterday to study the un-socialist art of economic management, to become apprentices of the 'bourgeois' experts. In other words, rather than bypass the stage of industrialisation, to begin doing the job for the capitalists (who failed to do it in their own time), and sometimes with their cooperation. From now on, the economic tasks moved slowly but steadily into the focus of the Soviet state. It took eight more years, however, before Stalin could scrap virtually all the sacred axioms of socialist emancipation in the name of 'socialist industrialisation'.

Once set on the road to industrialisation, the state faced not only the question of studying, acquiring and constructing modern technology, though this was an uphill task in itself. The other necessity – which stood in strident contradiction to the 'liberating' essence of socialism – was the imposition of the 'spirit of employeeship' on the listless mass of peasants and former peasants.

The incompatibility of intrinsically peasant attitudes and the logic of industrial employment has been widely described by sociologists and anthropologists. Though mostly concerned with the 'spirit of entrepreneurship', Max Weber dedicated a few trenchant pages to an analysis of the insensitivity of pre-industrial men to allurements which their descendants, having been appropriately processed and drilled, would perceive as stimuli for persistent and dedicated work. Pre-industrial man, we are told by Weber, did not ask 'how much can I earn if I work a specific amount of time?', but 'how long must I work to earn enough to meet the standard I enjoyed yesterday?' If pre-industrial man earned in a day enough money to satisfy his humble needs for two days running he saw no reason whatsoever for spending this second day in the factory. To transform the uninspired, monotonous and incomprehensibe factory work into a commonsensical routine, rarely if ever questioned, a protracted and pitiless drill was admittedly necessary, a unique mix of near-starvation wages with a lavish addition of non-economic pressures which went as far as direct physical coercion. The slave of Nature who had learned to copy Nature's slowly revolving annual cycles had to be remoulded into a slave of the machine and to accustom himself to its uncompromising rhythm.

This obviously paramount historical act was caught by the revolution practically in its very first stage. And the revolutionary power, if it meant industrialisation seriously, had to pick it up where the unfinished and abortive Russian capitalism had left it. It left it, as we know, far behind the aim envisaged by Marx in *Capital* (vol. III): 'The realm of freedom actually begins only when labour, conditioned by need and external necessity, ceases; there-fore, in the nature of the case, it lies beyond the sphere of particular material production.' The target which the revolutionary power in Russia had to reach before it could even contemplate a thrust toward the 'realm of freedom' was to develop precisely this 'par-ticular material production', which – according to Marx – was the realm of necessity, unfreedom, and perhaps unavoidable alienation. In his critique of the Gotha programme Marx insisted that the level of justice cannot rise above the level of material production and of the culture that this production conditions. This proved to be true, at least in retrospect, in the first socialist experiment. Lenin seemed to believe that the fact that the 'socialist' power presides over the process of constructing the material infrastructure would not bar it from preserving intact the final goal of liberation and disaliena-tion, and in due time handing over the socialist utopia, fresh and untarnished, to the generation resourceful enough to turn it into reality. On the fourth anniversary of the October revolution, Lenin advised the party: 'you must first of all strive to build the solid roads which, in a petit bourgeois country, will lead to socialism via state capitalism'. As it turned out later, it happened to be exactly the 'socialist power' which became alienated from the community of producers in the process. It was by no means clear how this alienated power, having established itself as a state capitalist system, could possibly commit suicide by dissolving itself in the 'free community of socialist producers' – the phrase Lenin considered a synonym for the socialist state.

It has been suggested by Alfred Meyer that the major concern, which was largely responsible for delineating the range of options and responses open to the Soviet power in its infancy, was the 'primitive accumulation of authority' – 'a desperate attempt to transform power into authority as quickly as possible'.[2] Again, there was hardly anything novel about a revolutionary group, which came to power by breaking the continuities of 'legitimacy', being preoccupied with buttressing its rule with an appropriate legitimation. The problem which confronted the Soviet power was unique in requiring the legitimation of the rule of an elite committed to modernity in a country which had never before generated a modern legitimation of power.

The pre-modern legitimation of state power is focused directly on the right of a ruler to rule; the ruler is seen as the repository and source of authority, and instead of needing confirmation of his rights from another social agent, he enjoys the unique capacity of confirming, by his will, the rights of all other agents to demand and to command. Whatever power is allocated to lower rungs of the authority ladder derives from the top. One of the major changes which took place with the advent of modernity is that described earlier as 'plebiscitarianism'. The ruler must now be confirmed by the people. Before the confirmation reaches the top it passes through a multitude of mediating stages, a dense network of social agencies which articulate (or generate what is taken as articulation of) the will of the people.

In other words, the modern state is sustained by the Gramscian 'civil society'. The network of social agencies mentioned above is nothing but the texture of civil society, filled with intellectuals, the professional 'articulators' of group interests and postulates. The political power is 'legitimate' in so far as the public philosophy generated, disseminated and inculcated by the agencies of 'civil society' supports the utopia which the political power of the state is committed to pursuing. The commitment to communal life, loyalty to the decisions declared in the name of the community, the readiness to obey the rules laid down in its name, are generated by the civil society and solidify into a firm foundation on which the drama of the political struggle for state power is staged. It precedes and supersedes the political divisions. It contains the political ruptures within the broad framework of popular 'in-group' feelings. Civil society, as noted earlier, links commonsense to the philosophy which guides state action. The administration of the society is then one of 'hegemony'. But the commonsense of the masses is satisfied that this administration is carried in its name only in so far as it remains linked to, or subjugated by, the ruling philosophy. Breaking the link, or weakening the subordination, transforms hegemony into domination, that is, the rule of the state, not undergirded by the fine tissue of civil society.

Though all sweeping historical generalisations are vulnerable one can say tentatively that in the West to a much greater extent than in Eastern Europe the advent of the modern state coincided in time with the emergence of a truly modern civil society. It is for this reason that the process of development of modern states in the West can be so often described as the rise of 'nation-states'. In a large part of Eastern Europe the nations, in the sense of elaborate civil societies built into linguistic and cultural communities, emerged within political states which spread far beyond the boundaries of the cultural community in question. The 'national problem', a typically Eastern-European concept and preoccupation, took from the start the shape of 'a nation in search of the state', a civil society in search of a political state to lean on and to support. Hence the bizarre and in many respects unique phenomenon of cultural hegemony at war with political domination. This was the case of Poland, of Hungary, of Bohemia, of the Southern Slavs, of the Baltic republics. This admittedly was not the case of Russia, and particularly not of its central, truly Russian, core.

This is not to say that the civil society tissue was not growing under cover of tsarist rule and, moreover, steadily gaining in ground and inner richness. But it is to say that, before tsarist rule was toppled, civil society had not advanced enough to gain a genuine constituency, to penetrate to a substantial degree the popular commonsense, to reach the level of the mass imagination and to assimilate the political state by adapting itself to its prerequisites. Until the very end of tsarist rule Russian civil society remained uncomfortably squeezed between the hammer of the autocratic tsarist bureaucracy and the anvil of inert and illiterate masses. More than once the autocrat appealed to the masses above the heads of the civil society's spiritual leaders, with most unsavoury consequences for the latter. When the criticism, simmering among the intellectuals, short-circuited with the dramatic eruption of popular anger, the leaders of civil society split into those who were prepared to organise into a new political state and those who were not prepared to supply the civil-society structure for this state. The first group slipped neatly into the traditional slot of the alienated, remote and omnipotent central political power; the second, at odds with all and any incarnation of political dominance, was promptly swept aside, if not destroyed, by the first. The 'family quarrel' between warring groups of equally dispossessed and powerless intellectuals was transformed into an all-out onslaught of one group, now identified with the political state, upon the other. In the result, the new body politic emerged from the revolutionary turmoil as a pure domination again, the state without a civil society.

The revolutionary elite which came to power and transformed itself into the political state did not see the emerging situation in this way. Its perspective was distorted by the fact that throughout its pre-revolutionary history it was an element of a potential civil society rather than an ingredient of the political structure of the state. Barred from real competition for state power, it considered itself mainly an intellectual force bent on arousing and articulating the dormant self-awareness of the dispossessed classes. The leaders were much more intellectual spokesmen than politicians in any 'institutionalised' meaning of the word. Predictably, they continued to see themselves as such long after they started, crudely and incompetently, to tinker with the issues of state power. They still deemed themselves mainly propagandists and tried to kindle mass enthusiasm as the only fuel the political engine may require, at least until they were replaced, imperceptibly at first, dramatically later, by a new generation of unfeeling and sometimes cynical experts in administration. Whatever role they played objectively, Lenin's generation of rulers would hotly protest if identified unilaterally with the state; even when praising the virtues of state power, they would reduce the state's functions to those of civil society rather than vice versa. Hence the odd idea that a single party can perform both functions – an organ of domination and the agent articulating the variegated interests of the masses – was psychologically understandable even if it could not withstand a closer scrutiny. Perhaps it could even pass the test of reality, if only the reality were different from the Russian. In the specific Russian reality of a narrow socialist-oriented group ruling a society whose immense majority was strongly and implacably anti-socialist, this 'conjuncture' could result only in the state assuming unqualified dominance and reducing the civil society, or meagre relics of civil society, to the role of a figleaf or a useless adornment.

Perhaps because they saw themselves primarily as intellectuals, the revolutionary leaders attached such importance to thought and considered ideas as the most explosive weapon which should be severely rationed and whose distribution should be controlled as meticulously as the possession of firearms. Through their rule, at least until the end of the 1920s, they allowed considerable freedom of discussion and formulation of ideas within their own ranks; but from the very start they never tolerated ideas opposing the essential righteousness of the socialist target, nor did they tolerate the bearers of such ideas. For this reason the possibility of a civil society growing from the 'grass roots' level was cut off. Without it, the whole political structure was vulnerable, and its hold on the society shaky and inconclusive. This was a situation of uneasy, grudgingly accepted armistice, with each side watching the other with a wary eye and settling for *ad hoc* compromise. The shoots of a civil society, feeble as they were, grew 'from the top' and stopped far short of the masses. The vehement debate waged by the party intellectuals was incomprehensible to something like 90 per cent of the population. So far as the peasants were concerned, their world, after the brief episode of a rapid expansion, retreated to the secure but cramped shelter of the village community or neighbourhood. The peasants were again the 'locals'; and the central powers, far from symbolising national unity, meant again primarily tax-and-procurements (*obrok*) collectors, draft agencies and militiamen. If in 1927 there was in Russia one party member for every forty manual and white-collar workers, but only one for every 600–650 peasants, that was due in large measure to the explicit or implicit unwillingness of the ruling socialist-oriented elite to 'pollute' the purity of the socialist utopia by an infusion of the petty-bourgeois world view which peasants epitomised. It was not an attempt to capture the peasants for socialism which failed; it was rather an inevitable effect of a deeply ingrained, rarely questioned belief that the peasantry is in, but not of, the socialist state, that it does not belong there, and that it appears in the socialist constellation of tasks only as an object, as a problem to be solved.

The first decade of the new state therefore hardly provided the conditions necessary for the emergence of a modern nation. It was not a nation-state then, nor was it on the way to becoming one. The rich and daring cultural creativity of the period failed, even before the final freeze set in, to reach beyond the confines of an esoteric intellectual circle; it was still an offer suspended in the air, largely irrelevant and incommunicado to both commonsense and the ruling philosophical idiom, and not even remotely approaching the status of a new national culture.

The next – Stalinist – period brought a total and implacable ban on all cultural experiments and the elevation of petty-bourgeois commonsense, now dubbed 'socialist realism', to the rank of the dominant cultural idiom. The most prominent mark of this period was denigration of the philosophical formula as a nation-integrating factor. The political state now assumed a complete, unqualified monopoly of systemic integration; abandoning (or deliberately renouncing) all hopes of the assistance which a closely-knit, full-blooded civil society might eventually offer, the state settled for a purely political, that is, coercive, means of sustaining the system. The role of the relics of the philosophical formula was reduced to that of magic incantations chanted on ceremonial occasions and never believed to be effective enough to relieve, much less to replace, the police functions of the state. The culture of 'socialist realism' was not meant to provide a link connecting this formula and commonsense, or to open the channel through which the formula could eventually permeate and remould the content of the latter; nor was it meant to generate gradually a new philosophical formula, which the system could in the end appropriate and transform into the idiom of cultural hegemony. The culture of 'socialist realism' was a culture of average taste, and the average tends to abhor and to eradicate the unusual, the novel, the out-of-the-ordinary, the utopian. The culture reduced to such commonsense is the culture of an atomised society, which mirrors its amorphism in being an aggregate rather than a system. As such, the culture of 'socialist realism' naturally complemented the all-powerful and totally alienated state. This culture underscored, and in some devious way sustained, the final rupture between the domain of the state and that of the individual; the communication between the two was now irrevocably broken. The apparent conquest of the cultural realm by commonsense meant the ignominious and ultimate defeat of the common people. They were bereft now of intellectual tools with which they could grasp, comprehend and critically assess their own predicament, shaped by the omnipotent political state whose presence and role was not expressible, much less made intelligible, in the idiom of the only available culture.

As a result, Soviet society in the first forty years or so of its history made little headway toward a modern nation-state. To be sure, it did experience important infrastructural transformations which created conditions more favourable to the formation, in the future, of a modern state. Bringing huge masses of the population into motion, broadening their horizons in purely geographical terms, erecting a political structure with built-in channels of mobility and command which really integrated the most remote regions (at least politically) into a state-wide system, were perhaps among the most fateful of the transformations. But the task itself remained un-fulfilled, and it is still far from clear how a 'socialist state' will cope with a historical requisite which otherwise has been met by capitalist rule. But the fact that the pre-October history left the task unfinished bore heavily on the options and choices of the socialist regime.

Friedland and Rosberg wrote of African socialism:

> Unlike the Western majoritarian conception of democracy, the African Socialist rejects 'the will of all' or the will of the majority and adopts the language of Rousseau: the 'general will', the 'will of the people'. In fact, many of the leaders of the inde-pendent nations of Africa see themselves as filling the role of Rousseau's 'Legislator'.[3]

This could be a description of the state of mind of the leaders of the October revolution in Russia and most of their revolutionary allies. Russia, as well as Africa half a century later, embraced the socialist ideology not as an extension and negation of, but as a substitute for, liberalism as the cultural idiom of capitalism.

Not only the idea that one can and should use 'public opinion' as a measuring rod of the government's wisdom and right to rule, but public opinion itself, appeared together with, and was established by, the bourgeois state. In the course of its development the 'people' were slowly but consistently brought into the orbit of the body politic as a collection of individuals, each exercising his own political rights in separation from the others and each entering the ultimate political balance as an autonomous constituent of the quantifiable effect. The idiom of 'plebiscitarianism' stands and falls by the assumption that the 'people', as the source of all sovereignty, consists of individuals and not of qualitatively distinct bodies. Thus, 'the general will' was reduced to the will of the majority and identified with it. The identification was ideologically based upon the fiction of freedom of expression and political action, allegedly already achieved and firmly appropriated (as well as exercised) by each and every individual of which the people was com-posed.

This fiction was blatantly untenable in societies which clearly consisted of corporations (*soslovie* in the Russian case; kinship lineage in the African) rather than individuals. The corporation was not reducible to its individual members; nor was its 'will' or 'interest'. The political game on the societal battlefield seemed to be played by large groups, each representing its own reason, rather than by scores of indistinguishable individuals, thoroughly stripped of their group attributes. Political parties in a developed capitalist society are viewed as a set of options offered above the heads of independent individuals, among which the individuals choose those which are deemed to cater more fully to their needs and wishes; political support, like everything else, is a matter of offer and demand, a game played by two mutually independent actors. Not so in societies which have not gone through the process of atomisation on the structural and the cultural plane. There, a political movement seems to grow directly from one or another part of the people, rather than being an extraneous opportunity offered to the people; it is the people themselves who grow into a political movement, who 'constitute themselves into a state'.

This idiom did not take for granted the people's presence on the political stage. On the contrary, their right of entry was the main object of political struggle; the people were expected to conquer and dominate the political stage as a group and its collective manifestation – 'the general will'. The politicians who constituted the party proper were perceived as the relatively more mature and articulate spokesmen of the people, as a vanguard which leads the way and clears it for the masses; the vanguard itself fought for the right of the people to speak and to be heard. This target could be attained only if the shackles which hampered the people's political activity were shattered. Freedom – *vola* (it was under this name that freedom entered the Russian populist vocabulary, and its semantic undertones bore heavily on the meanings attached to the relatively tamed, 'civilised' *svoboda*) – meant above all the liberation from oppression and exploitation, in which one large class held another, even larger class. It was a matter between groups, not a matter between an individual and a group.

In this sense Lenin, when fulminating against the Mensheviks' attempt to transplant the Western model of the political party onto Russian soil, spoke for the Russian reality. The real bone of contention – whatever the participants in the debate thought of it – was not the necessity of an underground conspiracy in a police state, but an entirely distinct meaning of the party as 'the people-on-the-move', the party whose existence is tantamount to the people constituting itself as a political force. This was a goal never pursued, either as a tangible end or as a cultural value, by the Western parties, as specialised political agencies which appeal to the people only to obtain the quantifiable legitimation to rule. Short of being thoroughly ploughed by a protracted dominance of bourgeois individualism, both structural and cultural, Russian soil could bear only parties whose strength, and sheer existence, was the direct and immediate function of the masses-in-historical-action. Having understood this, Lenin was little worried about the issues which constantly troubled the Western Marxists with a democratic conscience: how to keep pace with the masses, how to retain their support without losing by the same token a good deal of the party's revolutionary ardour. To him, the party was the people, or it was not a party at all. The job of the full-time members of the vanguard was to arouse the masses from their lethargy and keep the cinders smouldering until the masses are prepared to blow them into a revolutionary flame. The premonition that such a party may in turn become an oppressor of the masses hardly ever occurred to Lenin.

But this is precisely what happened when the government of the state was taken over by the party leaders. They believed that they did it in the name of the masses; the party's self-image, by no means at odds with the 1917 reality, as 'the masses in action', seemed to supply all the guarantees needed for the essential identity of the party with the liberation of the masses. *Vola* meant freedom of the workers and the peasants from tsarist bureaucrats and police, as well as from landlords' bullying and exploitation; and all this had been accomplished in one fell swoop. To be sure, the masses achieved freedom *qua* masses only; but then, their freedom *qua* individuals was never put clearly on the agenda of Russian history. The suppression of individual freedom was not the price the party paid for the liberation of the masses, since, subjectively as well as objectively, there was little to suppress. All these 'matter-of-course truths' only made it more difficult to notice, and easier to swallow, the revaluation of old truisms by the sudden identification of yesterday's horizon of hope with today's reality.

The long-established habit of spelling freedom and abolition of exploiting classes in one breath reflected the truth of the pre-revolutionary reality; the identification was true as a horizon, distinct from reality but exposing its proper structure; it was true as a programme, as a summation of possibilities, in so far as the protracted process of emancipation could not take off unless the hurdle of class dominance, with no time left for its transformation into hegemony, was brushed aside. The truth, however, was relative and was bound to be negated the moment reality was brought closer to the horizon. The same faith which galvanised the movement toward freedom when perceived as a historical perspective turned into a major brake on the same movement when presented as the description of the already-accomplished reality. In its new role it reduced the notion of freedom to its pre-plebiscitarian scale and thereby deprived the new reality of its own horizon, stultifying further historical movement. The subjection of the individual was transformed into the cultural idiom of the new domination. Once established, it could easily be utilised as the philosophical formula of a most ruthless suppression of the masses, as collections of individuals, in the name of the new ruling interests. As before, the Party drew much democratic comfort from its belief that it represented the properly understood interests of the masses; but these interests were now re-defined as the defence of the *status quo* instead of its critique; as rooted ultimately in reality instead of the horizon which may be arrived at only by leaving the 'here and now' reality behind. In other words, a belief which might be true as an element of utopia turned patently biased when used as a foundation on which to erect a new ideology. It could remain true only if it retained its critical edge. 'The people' is a term which is either meaningless or stands for a realisation of deprivation. Therefore, almost by definition, no conclusive social reality can be good enough to warrant its description as the accomplished embodiment of the people's interests.

The revindication of community was seen by the socialist utopia as an event crowning the long period of 'maturation' of an individualistic society, and simultaneously reconciling the developed individual interests with those of society. 'Jumping the queue', by sidestepping the stage of individuation, could lead only, as it did, to the complete subjugation of the individual by a totally alienated societal power. Naturally, it delayed for at least another historical era the creation of an anthropological situation in which the seeds of democracy could grow.

All three 'not-yets', built into the Russian social structure the moment the revolutionary change of government took place, combined to make the realisation of the socialist utopia highly unlikely. They presaged a further tightening of the screw of unfreedom, rather than opening new vistas for human liberty; furthermore, by identifying the new serfdom with the realisation of socialist dreams they could only discredit the socialist utopia and posit it as running counter to the cravings and yearnings generated by the continuing oppression of the capitalist society, as a wrong answer to the questions which the innate flaws of capitalism maintained on the political agenda.

What, in fact, took place in the Soviet Union was a modernising revolution, complete with industrialisation and urbanisation, nation-building, construction of a modern state towering over vast domains of public life, ruled by a narrow minority, with the masses engaged in their habitual everyday routine and rarely transcending the confines of commonsense. This modernising revolution, however, achieved at tremendous cost, took place before the eyes of a world already appalled by the consequences of its own past industrialist intoxication, and unlikely to take delight in the sight of a few more factory chimneys and a denser crowd at the factory gates. The same world could be bewildered and terrified when shown its own past cruelty at the same time as it prided itself on its compassion for human suffering, its observance of the inviolable rights of the individual and its advances on the road to personal freedom.

Two important qualifications are, however, in order. First, unless one is prepared to go all the way with the crudest structural determinism, it cannot be taken for granted that the presence of the three 'not-yets' rendered the outcome inevitable. The question whether there was another road is doomed to yield inconclusive answers only in so far as it remains in the realm of theory, or in so far as no practical answer is attempted. It seems that at some point the link between the situation and its cultural and social consequences did become inevitable, but only when mediated by the human decision to embark on a 'short-cut' industrialisation. From then on, the prevention of the civil society from emerging and popular democracy from taking root, the tightening grip of the political state over the society, all this and many other features often subsumed under the heading of 'totalitarianism', could indeed be portrayed as 'inevitable'. But, like most other 'inevitabilities' in history, this one was produced, even if inadvertently, by the choices made by humans from among the range of options circumscribed by the sediments of previous human choices, usually described as the historical legacy.

Second, not all witnesses of the Soviet 'great leap forward' reacted to what they saw with the dispiriting feeling of *déjà vu les résultats*;

not all were alerted and put on guard by the expense they viewed as intolerable. Many others were lining up for the miraculous springboard able to catapult them from the abyss of deprivation, which they considered less bearable than any imaginable costs. For them, the Soviet trip to the modern age, accomplished within the time span of one generation, was the major revelation of the century. The Soviet experiment did prove that the tasks of the capitalist revolution can still be performed in an age in which capitalists themselves will shun the ire which the costs of industrialisation may provoke. Whether this was *quod erat demonstrandum* when the socialist utopia took off as the counter-culture of capitalism is a different question.

The fact is that the utopia taken over from the 'mature' Soviet system by the fascinated witnesses who felt like following the pattern was far removed from the socialist utopia as delineated before. It is no longer a utopia situated on the other side of the industrialisation process, which socialism originally abandoned to the mercy (or, rather, to the mercilessness) of bourgeois domination. On the contrary, it is now a utopia of industrialisation as such; a capitalist utopia with no room for capitalists, a bourgeois utopia in which private tycoons of entrepreneurship have been replaced by the grey, smart conformity of the bureaucratic octopus, and risky initiative by secure discipline. On the other hand, the morality expounded and expatiated upon by the new utopia is bourgeois through and through. It extols, as if following to the letter the Protestant recipe, the virtues of hard work, austerity, thrift; it calls for an enthusiastic self-abandonment in work which bears no resemblance to the liberated, self-propelled creativity painted in bright humanistic colours by people as different as Marx and Weitling; it fulminates against idleness and disinterested enjoyment, equating them with an anti-social parasitism; it frowns upon shy mutterings about the individual's right to disobedience, for non-compliance with the rules of the game is a social sin and puts the sinner outside the community. It is, in short, a 'populist' version of the old bourgeois utopia, telescoping the tasks which the bourgeoisie performed in a comparatively leisurely, 'easy' way ('industrial spurt' in Gerschenkron's terms).

This truncating or trimming of the original bourgeois utopia, thereby adjusting it to the new shape of the industrialisation project (and the circumstances in which the project is to be implemented), has had its parallels in adjustments which became in the process the distinctive features of the Soviet social structure and of the Soviet state. A sharply pronounced stratification and the elimination of the masses from the political process unites them with their respective capitalist opposite numbers.

The essential polarisation of the capitalist social structure is founded on the market, which sediments, at opposite poles, 'the haves' and 'the have nots'; the former basing their supremacy on their control over fundamental constituents of the situation of the latter. They control access to the means of existence. Private ownership, which is the form their control assumes, is a negative rather than positive quality; the genuine meaning of 'I own it' is that everybody else is barred from using the objects of my ownership unless complying with conditions which I lay down. It happened that these objects (tools of production, raw materials, access to the merchandising outlets, etc.) are, in modern society with its intricate division of labour, the irreplaceable ingredients of the situation in which men can obtain a share in the socially distributed goods they need. Whoever controls these objects, therefore, holds in his hands paramount foci of uncertainty, and such control is tantamount to an effective power over the life and conduct of the less fortunate. In general terms, in each complex organisation the power which individuals or groups enjoy is measured by the sources of uncertainty they control; the more effective is this power, the more vital, for the other side, is the uncertainty in question; and the less 'uncertainty generating', that is, the more repeatable, monotonous and predictable are their reactions. The attempts to retain as much discretion and freedom of manoeuvre as possible are therefore coupled with efforts to impose the strictest possible regulation on the behaviour of others.

When viewed in this perspective, as a negative rather than positive attribute, ownership of the Soviet type (though admittedly not private) took over lock, stock and barrel the polarising qualities of capitalist ownership. The vast masses of the population are again barred from control over the objects which mediate their access to goods. There has been a total and consistent retreat from the initial, and – as it turned out – temporary situation, in which a number of vital goods were distributed without the mediation of the market. In particular, the immediate producers do not control the objects which they themselves operate. Since their life-situation is organically mediated by the objects in question they are not fully equipped to cope with the problems of their own life, unless they surrender to demands which condition their access to these objects. Their predicament is, therefore, essentially the same as in capitalist society; the same restrictions of their freedom and the same necessity of submission to an alien will are built into this predicament. The only meaning that can be given to the fact that ownership is 'common' and not 'private' is perhaps that even those people who control the access of others do not enjoy control over their own life-situation as fully as their capitalist opposite numbers.

The opposition 'controlling–being controlled' therefore polarises the Soviet social structure in the same way as it polarises the capitalist one. The vast majority of the population is here, as there, unambiguously on the 'controlled' side. The only way in which this majority can still generate uncertainty in their controllers' situation is in their freedom of producers' and consumers' choice, changing their employment or pattern of consumption if the supply in both fields is abundant, which is not always the case. Even in this limited area their range of manoeuvre is often reduced to a minimum, as in the case of the 'factory ascription' introduced at the height of the Stalinist dictatorship, or in times of rationing when consumers were forced to modify their diet according to somebody else's decisions. Even leaving such particularly odius episodes aside, producers' and consumers' freedom is still hampered in ordinary times by the institution of a continuous record of job performance, which must be produced at each place of employment, and which puts the worker at the mercy of his superiors. Most important of all, only individual means of manoeuvre and resistance are left to the controlled majority. From the 1920s and throughout most of Soviet history the controlled majority remained bereft of the means of collective defence, which are common in a fully developed capitalist society; its only bargaining position as a group stemmed from the fact that the controlling minority had to consider it as a more or less unified and compact category defined by distinct interests and, presumably, by limited endurance.

Control, on the contrary, has been collectivised. For roughly forty years of Soviet history the controlled majority, pulverised into a multitude of individuals, has been confronted with a well-integrated and usually united controlling group, again unlike the situation typical of a capitalist society. During these forty years the Soviet system combined, so to speak, the organisational unity of the controlling class, conceivable as a radical extrapolation of trends visible in highly developed capitalism, with atomism of the controlled class known from the early, largely pre-industrial history of capitalism. Alienation of the system from the largest class in society was consequently more complete and unadulterated than at any specific point in the 'natural history' of capitalism. The 'leadership' of the body politic, unified in the state-and-party organisation, provided the Gerschenkronian 'substitute' for the capitalist class without changing the essential pattern of polarization, but soliciting a greater, unqualified submission of society, required by the condition of an 'industrial spurt'.

In opposition to a diffuse, market-regulated economic growth, a planned economy is teleogically, rather than genetically, determined; its success depends on the degree to which the planners can secure the concerted action in one prescribed direction of all factors operative in the economy. The problem they put before themselves is not how to predict the conduct of these factors, which is, and presumably will remain, regularly monotonous, but how to engender the modification of its regularity in a desirable direction. The success of the plan depends, therefore, on the extent of the planners' command over the assets relevant to its implementation. The 'ideal plan' situation is, of course, a fiction, like the 'perfect market' model. Some assets will admittedly remain beyond planners' control unless the country in question achieves complete autarky and a total mastery over natural conditions, which is very unlikely. But because of the prerequisites of the model a temptation is built into any planning situation to submit to the planners' will and manipulation all the other assets which are tantalisingly accessible to the planners' control. Producers' and consumers' conduct are the first to fall natural victims of this temptation.

The task consists in breaking the autonomous regularity of conduct, which appears to the planners as tough, stubborn Nature which is to be defied and subdued. This can be achieved either by isolating the individuals from the pressure of 'ordinary' factors which undergird the undesirable monotony of their conduct, or by introducing new factors to counterbalance and minimise the impact of 'ordinary' ones, or both. The history of Soviet industrialisation has been full of such measures. Enforced collectivisation made food supplies largely independent of the peasants' reactions to the vacillation of terms of trade in general, to 'price-scissors' in particular, and radically widened the planners' freedom of manipulation. The forced labour conditions imposed upon Soviet industry made the workers' performance essentially independent of the game of material rewards. The permanent acute shortage of consumer goods deprived the vagaries of consumers' choice of any serious impact on the planners' freedom. Last but not least, the irrational, unpredictable terror became a supreme uncertainty in the situation of individuals and hence the paramount determinant of conduct, deflating all the other traditional factors.

The political state which took shape in the period of the industrial spurt differed in many respects from the structure which matured gradually in the course of Western, 'genetically determined' industrialisation. The pattern which emerged in the West and provided the dominant paradigm of Western political science was marked by an institutional separation between control (property) holders and the incumbents of political offices. The identity of interests and action between the two, even if assured in practice most of the time, was never given immediately and unproblematically; nor was it guaranteed by the very structure of the institutional network. Granted such historical experience as virtually the sole object of theorising, one would expect that the distinction between ends and means, protean and derivative as it was, would become, as it did, the essential theoretical model in most political theory. To Weber, the bureaucratic rule of 'dispassionate specialists' was a phenomenon fully accommodated within the realm of practice. In order to command the loyalty of the subjects, to acquire a sense of direction and purpose, and to measure and control its own performance, the Weberian bureaucracy needed to be headed by a leader who could lay out the ends and fix strategic goals precisely because he himself was not a bureaucrat. Thus, bureaucracy was not a viable entity unless subject to a 'will', generated by a charismatic leader, by a dominant class, or by 'popular representatives'. By itself, it was an empty vessel (as is everything 'rational' in Weberian thinking) which might be filled with virtually any content.

The intellectual impact of the Weberian idiom was so overwhelming that for a long time it hindered a proper understanding of the nature of the Soviet state. Under its sway political scientists tended to focus their attention on the person of the despot (or a despotic 'inner circle') as the real fulcrum of political structure, viewing the party as a largely executive appendix. This, in turn, hindered understanding of the post-Stalin period and caused many an analyst to embark on an endless and abortive guessing-game as to the identity of the next Stalin, instead of undertaking a realistic assessment of the party structure and functions and their continuity and change. The crux of the matter is that the ruling party in the Soviet Union, without losing its character as a large bureaucratic organisation, staffed by specialists, assumed the role of the source of legitimation, command, and goal selection. Law and administration, legitimation and the enforcement of authority, ends and means, *Wert* and *Zweck*, purpose and its attainment – all these irreconcilable oppositions of the Weberian analytical idiom – finally merge. Bureaucracy, so to speak, transcends itself by gaining the ultimate ascendancy and rendering the charismatic ruler (or for that matter any other purveyor of ends and values) redundant. Its transformation heralds the discarding of the strait-jacket of the servant-minded *Zweckrationalität*; it is not bureaucracy any more, if bureaucracy is what Weber outlined in his ideal type.

Paradoxically, it was Stalin – the very 'charismatic despot' of political scientists, who allegedly reduced the party to the level of Weberian bureaucracy – who first articulated this new concept of political rule, alien to the historical experience of the West. (It is true that he did it before he became the despot, in 1924).

> The party must absorb all the best elements of the working class. . . . The party is the general staff of the proletariat. . . . The distinction between the vanguard and the main body of the working class, between party members and non-party people, cannot disappear until classes disappear. . . . The party, as the best school for training leaders of the working class, is, by reason of its experience and prestige, the only organisation capable of centralising the leadership of the struggle of the proletariat, thus transforming each and every non-party organisation of the working class into an auxiliary body and transmission belt linking the party with the class.

'Working class' in this passage stands for the ultimate source of authority as selected by the revolution; but the statement itself is about 'absorbing into the party the authority itself and becoming its sole repository and interpreter'. Khrushchev would later substitute 'the people' for the working class; but the assumption that the party incorporates all mature, intelligent and informed elements of the social body in whose name it rules, and is thereby identical not only with the skill of politics, but with the wisdom of history, remained intact. Notice as well the abundance of military metaphors. As it were, the army has been rightly chosen as a prototype of a self-governing bureaucracy; the general staff in time of war sets these strategic goals and administers their implementation. The Soviet state in the period of the industrial spurt was an army at war, and the party captured the role of its general staff. Some think that the war was declared for the sake of this capture.

The gaining of ascendancy by a political bureaucracy has occurred more than once in human history, and in itself it does not convey the uniqueness of the Soviet experience. In general terms one can say that a situation propitious to the advent of bureaucratic rule arises whenever the dominant class is too weak, flaccid, or unsure of itself to sustain its hegemony in a matter-of-course way, by democratic self-government. In Gramscian terms, power and supremacy are directly related to the weakness of civil society, the insufficiency or absence of hegemony. The rule of the class which profits from the prevalent pattern of dependency and control can then be sustained only by dominance; and dominance means the expansion of the political state with bureaucracy as its substance. The essence of bureaucratic rule is alienation of the citizen's role, of political control over the conditions in which the relations of dependency are established and preserved. In other societies, in which several sources of power exist in relative separation from each other, this alienation of political control – though it may seem to afflict all classes in equal measure – handicaps most severely those classes which are put in a subordinate position by other, non-political forms of power relation. In this sense, the alienation of political control strengthens and protects the alienation of control over other spheres of social life, particularly over work and communication.

The important point, however, is that even if bureaucracy gains independence in its administrative performance, the substance of this administration does not; the content of political alienation is determined by the non-political power structure, and in this sense bureaucracy may indeed be described as a neutral, non-partisan rule of experts. The non-partisanship means precisely that it is not the experts who decide or even discuss the ends of the ruling process. The ends are already there; they are neither generated, nor consciously fought for by the bureaucracy. On the contrary, they persist and perpetuate themselves precisely because of the bureaucratic neutrality and value indifference.

On the other hand, thanks to its own political alienation the dominant class gains a large measure of independence from the state. The intra-class power structure may be heavily affected by

D

the favours or hostilities of the state administration; but class dominance as such remains relatively secure. The ruling bureaucracy is not, so far as the dominant class is concerned, a source of all-important uncertainties, and therefore it does not gain supremacy over class dominance. In the same way as the ruling bureaucracy controls individual members of the dominant class to ensure class dominance as such, this dominance, based upon non-political factors, controls and limits the political rule of bureaucracy. This evidently does not apply to the Soviet system. In Isaac Deutscher's words, 'if under the capitalist system we say that the power of bureaucracy always found a counterweight in the power of the propertied classes, here we see no such restrictions and no such limitations.'[4]

Weber's ideal type, this supreme sublimation of the Prussian bureaucracy steering uneasily between junkers and bourgeoisie, each unable to tip the balance in its favour, stops at the threshold of the Soviet experience. With the abolition of private ownership the most powerful non-political sources of power disappear, and bureaucracy shares its supremacy over the society with nobody. Its only 'counterweight', as we saw earlier, is the diffuse and in-articulate powers of individual producers and consumers, the general limits of human endurance and readiness to conform with routine patterns of conduct. All dimensions of alienation are thus subsumed in the unified process of political alienation. This makes the ruling bureaucracy more powerful than any other known historical case. But the cause of its omnipotence is, at the same time, its undoing. The dominance of the Soviet system is all of a piece, is all in the political dimension, and has no further lines of fortifications to fall back upon. In Soviet conditions, a political reform, if only it is thorough enough, may completely change the whole pattern of dominance. There is no further 'depth' beyond the ruling bureaucracy, no vast domain of civil society in which the utopian zeal of so many political revolutions petered out.

Having eradicated democracy from the political process to an extent unknown before, bureaucratic supremacy is more vulnerable to democratic assaults than any other historical form of dominance. In most cases the passage to relatively more democratic forms of political rule signified the growing rootedness and self-reliance of the economically dominant class. It is only in the case of the Soviet bureaucracy, at present embodied in the partynomial system,[5] that democratisation may bring about a veritable upheaval in the structure of dominance. Whatever group or category of the society gains access to the political game obtains by the same token its share in dominance. It is mainly for this reason that politics, having been equated with societal dominance as such, becomes the sole vehicle of any systemic change. On this peculiar property of the Soviet system some writers (Deutscher perhaps being the most prominent) base their view that despite the most abject suppression of freedom, the Soviet system is somewhat closer to socialism (or, rather, offers less resistance to a genuinely socialist transformation) than economically more developed capitalist societies. Several conditions must be met, however, for this possibility to become realistic. One is the elimination of scarcity which, at least on the everyday plane, makes men slaves to their own banausic activities. The second is the emergence of a civil society which, in Soviet conditions, will mean the maturation of self-government. This maturation depends in turn on the masses rising to the level of political consciousness.

In other words, the fact that the Soviet system is less distant from a system approximating the socialist vision than capitalist countries can only become evident, as well as true, if the Soviet system succeeds in completing the task of the capitalist revolution. Thus far, the appropriation of the socialist label by a regime bent upon industrial take-off in conditions requiring an unheard-of aggravation of human suffering, serfdom and alienation has had an adverse effect on the popularity of the socialist utopia in the industrial world. In Deutscher's words again, 'the revolution in a precapitalist society, which nevertheless aspired to achieve socialism, produced a hybrid which in many respects looked like a parody of socialism. . . . The Russian revolution has acted as a deterrent to revolution in the West.'[6] The most harm, however, has been done by the Russian revolution to the cause of the socialist utopia in the industrial world, not on the plane of invidious comparisons of the standard of living, efficiency, technological prowess etc., but on the plane of the positive values the Soviet system preached under the auspices of socialism. The power of socialism, as we saw before, consisted in its status as the counter-culture of capitalism, and in its role as a thoroughly critical utopia, exposing the historical relativity of capitalist values, laying bare their historical limitations, and thereby preventing them from freezing into an horizon-less commonsense. The ideology adopted by the Soviet system and then fed back into the capitalist world with all the initial authority of the 'first socialist country' was, on the plane of essential values and ethical system, a complete reversal of these premises. The transient bourgeois values of progress measured by the number of factory chimneys, work discipline, puritan morality, were portrayed as universal laws of historical development and attributes of ultimate human perfection. The Soviet system came to measure its own perfection and its own progress in the 'building of socialism' with the help of a bourgeois measuring rod. At the same time it joined forces with the most conservative bourgeois counter-utopia in denouncing the aim of dis-alienation and the popular demand for control, which had constituted the uniqueness of the socialist utopia.

In consequence, to the extent that the Soviet system was successful in influencing the frame of mind of the socialist forces in the West, it strengthened the grip of the bourgeois hegemony over commonsense. It contributed to an unqualified support for the concept of progress measured in GNP, to the reduction of human problems to those of economic efficiency, to erasing the problem of alienation from the agenda of human liberation, to restricting the international problem of freedom to the narrow frame of national sovereignty, and to a reinforcement of the state in its alleged role as the sole lever of human emancipation. The critical impact of its presence in the essentially capitalist world, and its outspoken subscription to the socialist ideology, have been limited to a basically sympathetic critique, fully expressible in the language of bourgeois commonsense, which by pointing out the most egregious and festering afflictions of the capitalist system facilitated, and sometimes forced, their timely correction. It is perhaps a consequence of the appropriation of the socialist designation by the Soviet system that, in Maximilien Rubel's words, 'Dans les conditions du monde d'aujourd'hui, la présence de Marx s'impose donc plus par la critique et la dénonciation du faux socialisme que par la théorie du vrai capitalisme, ancien et nouveau, occidental et oriental'.[7]

7

Socialism as Culture

In the last analysis, the attempt to build a socialist society is an effort to emancipate human nature, mutilated and humiliated by class society. In this crucial respect the Soviet experiment conspicuously failed. If censured for the apparent inability to catch up with the more spectacular Western measures of affluence, the Soviet system can always point to the appallingly backward starting-point, to the indisputable lessening of the distance dividing it from its capitalist competitors, and to many achievements in eradicating the most extreme forms of material poverty. No excuses, however, can be mustered for the servility and obsequiousness of the 'new socialist man', Soviet style. The harshest of modern totalitarian regimes created, as its lasting product, men and women terrified by the prospect of freedom, unused to having views, to defending them, and to accepting responsibility for their convictions. The 'ideal Soviet man' turned out to be the petty-bourgeois average man writ large. The petty bourgeois mistaken for 'socialist man' is organically incapable of imagining an existence different from his own, and therefore all criticism portends a replacement of his present security, however meagre and shabby, by the uncharted, and so terrifying, waters of history.

Hence the most comprehensive and ambitious of socialist experiments to date has little to offer in the way of an alternative to the capitalist-inspired culture. That staunch and unwavering Marxist, Georg Lukács, it was rumoured, regarded the inability to generate a new alternative culture as the ultimate failure of the Soviet socialist experiment. This failure has been the direst of all the misfortunes which the socialist utopia has suffered in the two centuries of its history. *Homo consumens*, brought up on the breath-taking raptures and nerve-breaking tensions of the capitalist market, finds little attraction in the paltry 'socialist' equivalent which offers the same tensions of endless commodity chase but little joy of acquisition. *Homo creator*, who finds the inert indifference of capitalist commonsense oppressive, can hardly be inspired by the sight of a similarly impervious commonsensical routine, crowned with undisguised and rapaciously conservative coercion.

The Soviet version of socialism offers in the field of culture little more than a brand of capitalism grossly inferior to its Western counterpart. The sole measure, on both sides of the barricade, is output per head, efficiency per unit of capital and per working hour, availability of commercialised paraphernalia, a 'full life' defined as the volume of private possessions etc.; and Soviet socialism contrives to offer such standards at a time when the West is increasingly weary and apprehensive of 'material' adornments that capitalism offers, or may offer, to human life. Having defined itself as a more adroit runner in the race along the capitalist track, Soviet socialism has condemned itself, at best, to the role of the poor country's substitute for the ordinary levers of the capitalist cultural revolution, and at worst has committed itself to the attempt to freeze the capitalist cultural formula to an extent that 'ordinary' capitalism never managed to achieve. Far from opening the windows of history on breathtakingly vast expanses of human freedom, Soviet socialism failed to achieve even the qualified and truncated personal liberty which the liberal formula of capitalist culture delivers. Even for a well-wisher, who will be prepared to play down labour camps and witch-hunts as temporary and untypical mishaps, the volume of freedom built into the everyday routine of Soviet life must look shoddy and pitiful. No wonder that the Soviet experiment, if it proved that the socialist utopia is 'realistic' and accessible, deprived it simultaneously of any attraction. If, on the other hand, the experiment can be explained away as a product of bizarre and unique contingencies it becomes irrelevant to the question of the feasibility of this utopia.

Contrary to many socialists' expectations, the development of capitalism, far from precipitating a naked and brutal confrontation between classes, has brought about a replacement of domination by hegemony; a process which Antonio Gramsci, with his remarkable insight, foresaw half a century ago. The stability of capitalism acquired a cultural foundation. This means that the ideals of a good life, accepted ends of action, wants perceived as a reflection of needs, cognitive schemata which organise world perception, and above all the way in which the borderline between the 'realistic' and the 'utopian' has been drawn, sustain and perpetuate the totality of capitalist relations with little or no interference by the political state. It means also that whatever change may take place within the realm of the state, the capitalist type of human relations is unlikely to give way unless driven away by new culture. As Fromm put it, 'fantasy satisfactions' generated and inculcated by capitalism 'serve as a substitute and become a powerful support of social stability',[1] a stability strong enough to withstand and outlast a reshuffling of the ruling elites.

Unless attacked at its roots the hegemonic capitalist culture demonstrates an enormous survival capacity, which Marx failed fully to appreciate. Gramsci was perhaps the first Marxist thinker to understand capitalism's vitality and resilience, and to sound the tocsin of the cultural revolution. Marxism, as Gramsci saw it, was 'beginning to exercise its own hegemony over traditional culture, but the latter, which is still robust and above all is more refined and finished, tries to react like conquered Greece, to stop the crude Roman conqueror from being victorious'.[2] It seems that the idea which 'capitalist Greece' implanted in the 'Roman socialist' mind was above all that of incessant and unlimited growth of production and productivity as the ultimate measure of human progress. In this remarkable achievement capitalism was greatly helped by the Soviet sleight-of-hand which subordinated the totality of socialist ideas to one all-embracing effort of industrialisation, designated the field of economic efficiency as the decisive battleground between capitalism and socialism, and reduced the case against capitalism to that of alleged inefficiency which a state-managed economy would supposedly eliminate. The broad humanistic ambitions originally attached to the idea of common ownership (reduction of toil, elimination of drudgery and inequality, liberation of the producer from his subordination to the machine, making labour pleasant and creative, restoration of control to the producers, overcoming of alienation etc.) have gradually been shelved, if not abandoned or branded as heresy.

At the same time, the original socialist measures have been assimilated and domesticated by the capitalist culture. Largely under the sway of Keynesian reformulations the survival of capitalism has been redefined in terms of the production of needs and the expansion of consumption. It was only to be expected that socialism, as the opponent of capitalism in the race laid out by the host's culture, would follow suit and hasten to redefine its challenge. Stalin threatened to surpass capitalist countries in the total output of industry; for Khrushchev, 'surpassing' meant high consumption of milk and meat. And the Western socialists, institutionalised in ruling parties or parties aspiring to rule, rarely look beyond the provision of a greater share of the consumer market for the handicapped. There is no challenge to the basic tenets of capitalist culture in the most powerful versions of the socialist utopia of today. Not that socialism lost its teeth; but capitalism has made itself immune to much of their bite. It has become an indelible mark of the hegemonic culture to view blatant inequality as injustice, human misery as society's fault, and to accept the right of the underdog to defend himself and to have a vital say in running his own affairs. This should be written to the credit of triumphant socialist utopia. By the same token, however, the traditional version of utopia lost much of its power of the critical conscience of reality.

The memory of socialism as a cultural project genuinely opposed to the dominant culture of capitalism is, of course, still alive. The tradition of cultural challenge from the position of socialism has, however, been evicted from the field of political struggle and has found its refuge in a largely intellectual cultural criticism. This divorce between cultural challenge and socialist politics has been expressed, though in somewhat perverted form, by Perry Anderson, as a situation in which socialism's 'comprehension, and its critique, of capitalist civilisation have made significant advances. In striking contrast, however, its strategic thought remains almost as weak as ever'.[3] The fact that the critique of capitalist civilisation, however penetrating and intellectually overpowering, remains hanging in the air while socialist policy quietly continues its normal course of curing the minor ailments of capitalist society cannot be blamed, of course, only upon the backwardness of strategic thought. It will take much more than another intellectual discovery to make utopia an element of political practice. The antinomy is longstanding and genuine. It lies at the root of the present crisis of socialism.

One can hardly disagree with George Lichtheim that 'if socialism means anything, it means the end of inequality and the substitution of non-economic goals for the aim of wealth accumulation'. Indeed, socialism amounts to the proclamation of man's emancipation from necessities imposed by the acceptance of accumulation of wealth as the guiding rule of human affairs. But if this is the essence of the socialist challenge, then its modern expression will be the hope that 'socialism will enable society to put a brake upon constantly growing productivity, rather than the other way round'.[4] This, however, is precisely a plank which no 'realistic' political party, looking for a working majority and prudently defining social consciousness as the opinions of voters, will wish to nail to its platform. The political competition for votes and parliamentary seats can only be carried on in terms of who gets how much of the values the hegemonic culture has to offer. It is obviously not a game designed for the struggle between alternative cultures. A party which persists in being oblivious to this truth is destined for suicide; in practice, it is more often than not stopped on its way to self-destruction by 'realistic rethinking' well before the point of no return has been reached.

The dilemma is as old as the Aristotelian distinction between *telos* and *nomos*. The first is what ought to be, the repressed and hidden potential of the living entity, its unachieved but possible perfection; the second is precisely the external force which bars the ideal state from being achieved, which keeps it repressed and cuts its wings just when they begin to stretch. Since its formulation by Aristotle, the dichotomy was ubiquituously present in the Western intellectual universe, though it assumed ever-new linguistic disguises. In the socialist tradition, perhaps two of the masks were particularly relevant: the dialectical contradiction between the dynamism of labour and the innate conservatism of property, as elaborated by Saint-Simon, and the Marxian clash between open-ended, inner-propelled human activity and the deadly grasp of the institutionalised products of alienation. Marx, in fact, never came anywhere near to showing how the first can, much less must, gain an edge over the second. In a sense, *Capital* makes depressing reading; it demonstrates, perhaps, why the capitalist system may eventually collapse under the burden of its own systemic incongruencies, but it hardly makes a convincing case for the *necessity* of human freedom establishing itself as an uncontested factor of human history, or of the 'active man' doing away with the shackles of alienated institutions. On the contrary, one learns from *Capital* that alienation is a self-perpetuating process and that the only necessity it creates is the necessity for the individual to surrender or perish. Sedulously and methodically Marx unravels the secrets of the power structure continually re-establishing itself through the sheer perfunctory repetitiousness of human commonsensical activities. Sociological 'laws' are concepts applicable to the

D*

materialised sediments of alienation; but it is intractable spontaneity which describes the nature of de-alienating human activity.

The closest the socialist revolution comes to historical necessity is in the vision of the tendencies of capitalism to cause unbearable suffering for the great masses of the pauperised proletariat and thereby push them to revolt. But even if this vision comes true it is still unclear why this revolt should necessarily be socialist in character. There has already been a revolution caused by the despair of pauperised masses, but it is open to question, to say the least, how close it has come to the realisation of the socialist utopia. Enlightened as we are by our historical experience, we are inclined to agree with Coser and Howe that 'given scarcity, there arises a policeman to supervise the distribution of goods; given the policeman, there will be an unjust distribution'.[5]

Now scarcity is an objective-subjective phenomenon, a result of projecting the culturally supplied expectations onto the socially offered opportunities. There is ample evidence of societies which, having much less to offer their members than we consider now to be a bare minimum, still managed to put man-made constraints on such increases of supply which, given the technology and resources available to them, were potentially within their reach. Capitalism, however, stands and falls by the continual re-creation of scarcity. Culturally, the experience of scarcity is an inexorable by-product of the acquisition of objects regarded as the only mode of personal self-actualisation and the only compensation for the humiliations of a down-graded social position. Socially, the experience of scarcity, like pain for a biological organism, becomes a crucial warning and orientating device in a situation in which the constant human need for certainty and security must be satisfied in the conditions of a market-regulated environment. Economically, production of ever-new 'relative deprivations' to replace the satiated ones, keeps the economy, based on profit and the market, afloat. We can surmise, therefore, that the policeman and unjust distribution are firmly and solidly anchored in the type of society which has been brought into being by the capitalist economy and which is sustained by the bourgeois culture.

The rub lies, however, in the fact that once such a type of society has come to pass in one part of *oikoumene*, the policeman and unjust distribution have also become a permanent feature of those societies which either wish to remain outside, or attempt to break out of the vicious circle of self-perpetuating scarcity. Even if it is not exacerbated by the local culture, the experience of scarcity is bound to emerge as a result of the cross-cultural and cross-societal demonstration effect, breeding relative deprivation. Any attempt to ward off the inevitable outcomes of cultural diffusion or to stop the triumphant advance of the market, will not do without a policeman and will surely create a distribution which will be seen as unjust. An economy which refuses to cater for insatiable scarcity will be considered a failure and will cause resentment. Scarcity, the policeman and unjust distribution share with each other their self-perpetuating flair.

Whether culture can be held responsible for the emergence and entrenchment of the above triad is a contentious matter which can hardly be discussed fully here. But without begging the question of origin we can safely assume that cultural hegemony of a specific kind is one of the key factors responsible for this triad's remarkable capacity to survive and to emerge unscathed from the most severe historical contingencies. Hence another assumption; that the future of socialism will be decided in the cultural sphere.

This realisation does not make any easier the life of thinkers concerned with the formulation of the socialist utopia of the late twentieth century which a century earlier was straightforward and, so to speak, transparent. One thing that socialism vociferously demanded then was that capitalism should deliver according to its promise. There was no need to build from scratch the case for technological progress, for the rule of rationalism, for the rights of the individual. Socialism was above all a critique of the failure of capitalism to put its theory into effect. The bourgeois culture, in a sense, provided a firm foundation and convincing reason for its socialist counterpart. This is no longer the case. The originally utopian ideas came close enough to their materialisation to cast doubt on the supposition that a radical emancipation of man can be achieved while pursuing consistently the values which capitalism brought to a head. To be sure, there is still a wide gap between socialist demands and willing or grudging capitalist concessions; and no welfare state can bring social equality anywhere near the socialist ideal. But the gap has been narrowed to the point at which one can see from one coast clear outlines of the other; and what one sees is much less inspiring than one used to hope. The other shore still seems far from the emancipatory ideal.

In striving toward consistency and realism the traditional socialist utopia was greatly helped by the hegemonic bourgeois culture. It can no longer count on this help. The socialist utopia has brought contemporary society as far as possible while acting within the framework circumscribed by what has come to be known as the industrial society. The next step, if there is one, will lead into the great Unknown. Beyond the welfare state, powerful trade unions, redistributive legislation, nationalised industries, vast, unexplored expanses stretch, on which the next battle of emancipation will be fought. And this is perhaps the major cause of the present strength and the present weakness of socialism. Its traditional tenets now acquired a powerful foothold in social reality itself and socialism is no longer forced to argue from the purely utopian position. But unless it is prepared to accept the role of one of the functional brands of hegemonic culture serving the existing society, and thus renounce the role of a utopian horizon-breaker, socialism has to begin again from the roots, from a re-analysis of essential and unquestioned values on which reality is grounded. And this time the hegemonic culture can offer little guidance. The present crisis is therefore deeper than anyone has experienced in the history of modern socialism.

The feeling of perplexity, only to be expected at the first encounter with a virgin frontier which nobody has yet bothered to furnish with signposts and warning lights, has been succinctly expressed by Norman Birnbaum: 'What we face is a situation of genuine historical indeterminacy.'[6] Well, all historical situations are indeterminate or, at least, insufficiently determined. They vary only in the degree to which their actors, first, consider the *status quo* as problematic, and second, are *themselves* determined to change it in a specific direction. The experience of indeterminacy is of course an attribute of its thinking actors, and results from the presence of the first factor and the conspicuous absence of the second. The utopia-producers ran out of ideas. Some of these ideas lost a lot of their lustre by descending dangerously close to the level of commonsensical triviality, while others were tried and then abandoned because they did not live up to previous expectations. But new and untried ideas are in short supply – not because our times are less lavishly furnished with perceptive minds and inventive intellects than the aftermath of the French Revolution, but because the task of our contemporaries is incomparably more complex. It will not do now as it did at the beginning of the nineteenth century to put the yardstick of exacting moral principles to values which, as everybody agreed, embodied the highest achievements of mankind and represented its future. Such values no longer exist. To put it briefly, the task of the producers of utopia consists now of creating a new culture, instead of criticising, challenging and correcting the existing one. Hence the feeling of indeterminacy.

This feeling is further aggravated by the realisation that the grip in which the hegemonic bourgeois culture holds popular commonsense is powerful enough to withstand such inroads as may be incited by the inner flaws and frailties of the present society; it is powerful enough to prevent, for a long time yet, such popular resentment as may erupt from flowing over the brim of the new hegemonic culture. Socialism launched its first assault against capitalism when the latter could not yet claim complete cultural hegemony. The cultural norms of capitalism were then more postulates than patterns of commonsensical routine, and thus enjoyed a status not qualitatively different from that of the socialist norms. Cross-pollination was therefore possible, and in fact did occur in the course of time. Since then, however, the bourgeois culture, enriched with such contributions from the socialist counter-culture as forced their way into its central value cluster (only to be assimilated and domesticated), has gained complete ascendancy over commonsense and has posited itself as the monopolistic spokesman for reality, realism and rationality. The task of the socialist utopia does not consist now solely of arguing how tomorrow should differ from today. It must first prove that tomorrow should and can indeed be different. In doing this it has routine, commonsense, and the dominant culture among its enemies. To an extent never known before it points 'to the possibilities which the *status quo* negates'.[7]

One can say that the history of socialism has come full circle. It started, in the work of Mably, Morelly, Saint-Simon or Fourier, as an idea in search of a constituency; it has become recently a constituency in search of an idea. The constituency consists of people who are aware of suffocating in the stale stench of the cul-de-sac into which the hopes stirred by the advent of industrialism have carried them; but they hardly know what the fresh air they need would be like or where to obtain it. As Wright Mills, with his usual perceptiveness, put it,

nowadays men often feel that their private lives are a series of traps. They sense that within their everyday worlds, they cannot overcome their troubles, and in this feeling, they are often quite correct. . . . Suppose they are unaware of any cherished values, but still are very much aware of a threat? That is the experience of *uneasiness*, of anxiety, which, if it is total enough, becomes a deadly unspecified malaise. Ours is a time of uneasiness and indifference – not yet formulated in such ways as to permit the work of reason and the play of sensibility'.[8]

These words were written fifteen years ago. And we still wait for such articulation of anxiety as may pave the way for reason and sensibility.

The feeling of being in a trap is not enough, however, to raise those affected out of their predicament. At most, it can furnish the energy of disaffection needed for the change. But it must be guided and channelled; it must be given a name which relates individual suffering to the supra-individual roots of unhappiness. As James O'Connor put it, one has to merge thought with feeling.[9] Neurotic fears born of the contradictions of late industrial society can be forged into the willingness to construct a new, alternative society only if an alternative hegemonic culture, the utopian foretaste of the society to come, saps the very foundation of the present one, its commonsense.

And so the constituency of thinkers is at pains to identify and put on record any hint and clue, however feeble and protean, of the better world to come. As might be expected, they try to unravel deeper meanings and lasting innovations in actions of despair, informed by feelings alone. Hippie movements and ghetto rebellions, however episodic they may have been, were the obvious candidates; they proved to be powerful enough levers, on the depressingly flat plain of meek routine, to hoist many a Roszak and a Reich to historiosophical heights, from which middle-class nausea and hunger riots could pass for a modern *Theleme*. Nostalgically, Martin Nicolaus wrote in 1967: 'It may well be that the hippies are to be *philosophes*, Allen Ginsburg and Abbie Hoffman and Paul Krassner, the Rousseau and the Diderot and the Voltaire, of a new American Revolution.'[10]

Sometimes more serious attempts were made to articulate the cultural principles of the transient hippie or sit-in communities, on the assumption that they represent, even though timidly and tentatively, glimpses of alternative forms of society. So it has been pointed out that the hippies transcended the split into subjects and objects of action, into actors and observers; that they defied compulsive consumption and flatly refused to work for a living; that they have overcome in practice the plague of commodity fetishism, re-establishing direct and undisguised relationships between human beings; that they escaped the impersonal mastery of time and restored human will (or whim?) as the sole factor structuring the logic and sequence of human deeds. The circumstance that hippies could achieve this only because other people did work for themselves and for others, agreed to be ruled by impersonal time etc., was prudently left without commentary, along with the troubling question whether a marginal and dependent cultural experiment of a consuming, but not producing, community can ever become the universal norm of a self-sustaining society. Some people, however, approached the task more judiciously, cogently arguing the need to analyse the bizarre and out-of-the-ordinary as explorations of repressed human potentiality, without begging the question of the direct relevance of these improvised solutions to the sought-for cultural alternative. Thus, Harry S. Kariel[11] challenged political scientists to perceive student rebellions and urban riots, strikes and demonstrations, marches of the poor, as structured dramas, as political projects which create meanings, as controlled efforts to break with actuality and display a new reality. Even if they are extemporising and groping in the dark, their participants may be acting rationally, though the frame of reference and the code of this rationality may escape us.

Daring or timorous, far-flung or cautious, all these attempts have one thing in common: they all start from the assumption that the guiding ideas of the new culture can no longer be found within the commonplace and the ordinary. Something much more far-reaching than just a reshuffling or rearrangement of the bits and pieces of reality is necessary. Neither the objective of making everybody as well-to-do as the rich of today, nor that of elevating inner-factory planning to the societal level, raises high expectations about the degree of human happiness and human emancipation that it may bring. So the utopia-seekers of today look beyond the boundaries at which their predecessors used to stop. The advanced socialist thought of today is breaking new horizons, reaching beyond the historical limits fixed by the industrial epoch for both bourgeois culture and its traditional socialist counter-culture. This widely shared belief has found its radical expression in the words of Marcuse:

What is at stake in the socialist revolution is not merely the extension of satisfaction within the existing universe of needs. . . .

The revolution involves a radical transformation of the needs
and aspirations themselves, cultural as well as material; of
consciousness and sensibility; of the work process as well as
leisure. This transformation appears in the fight against the
fragmentation of work, the necessity and productivity of stupid
performances and stupid merchandise, against the acquisitive
bourgeois individual, against servitude in the guise of technology,
deprivation in the guise of good life, against pollution as a way
as life.[12]

Ventures into counter-culture are not, of course, the only meaning that used to be associated with the concept of socialism in the
contemporary world. Even leaving aside the Soviet socialism of
unfreedom and alienation there is at least one more, and still
dominant, meaning which some years ago inspired Judith N.
Sklar to the following gloomy reflections:

> Success is probably an important cause of the theoretical decline
> of socialism. Sidney Webb's prediction that the 'slow and gradual
> turning of the popular mind' was toward socialism has been
> realised. Everyone is a bit socialist today, especially in England.
> Consequently there is no room for a specifically socialist philo-
> sophy. That too was the fate of liberalism. Success has meant that
> socialism has lost much talent. As long as it was the champion
> of the dispossessed, it could count on the artistic and polemic
> support of many romantic minds anxious to join the battle against
> the philistines. Once these artists discovered that a socialist state
> would do no more for them than any other, their ardour cooled
> markedly, and the revival of purely aesthetic romanticism began.[18]

Indeed, romantic, utopia-creating minds, explorers of distant,
invisible lands, could hardly be inspired by a struggle for human
consciousness which boiled down to the cajoling of floating voters,
or a battle for justice reduced to bargaining for an extra pound in
exchange for the acceptance of unfreedom. Socialism paid the usual
price of a successful utopia; having ceased to inspire imagination
(this imagination against which, according to Hegel, no actuality
can hold out), it has lost its power of supervising the next stage
of the human search for perfection. It has gained a firm grasp of
reality, it has penetrated commonsense, but in the process it has
lost its visionary capacity.

Thus attempts to emancipate utopian imagination from the shallow sands of daily realism tend inevitably to stray into the hanging gardens of moral and artistic criticisms. Between these two poles lie today the strategic dilemmas of modern socialism. Efforts to plug the gap between these poles constitute 90 per cent of the debate on the meaning of socialism in the contemporary world. The same conflict is lurking behind the tendency of so many critics of modern society to disavow their socialist connection.

8

Continuity and Change

In view of the loss of vigour of traditional socialist ideas, and the rising popularity of social and cultural criticism only loosely related to the contents of the original socialist utopia, can one still cover such disparate phenomena with a single term? Can one assume the continuity of a socialist faith extending over two centuries and reaching the world of today?

That the answer to this question is by no means unequivocal, can be seen from the caution, if not reluctance, with which many a radical critic of bourgeois culture agrees to use the concept of socialism to describe his own provenance. Indeed, contemporary ideologues of revolutionary change shun furnishing the revolution they profess with any adjective defining its direction; virulent and merciless as they are in censuring the *status quo*, they remain remarkably dumb as to the class anchorage or the principles of social organisation of the post-revolutionary society. Disenchanted with previous sallies of the socialist utopia into political realities, they only too willingly cede the banner of socialism to the institutionalised standard-bearers. Even those who do not want to relinquish the banner hasten to make clear that it has been so far put to the wrong uses, or that its colours were bleached by careless treatment and urgently need re-painting. 'Social democracy', writes Anderson, 'represented a false adaptation [to its world]. It appeared to be appropriate for its time and place, but this was not a genuine adaptation, it was in fact an *absorption*.'[1] To salvage the continuity of the utopia, one has to deny the continuity of practice which the utopia inspired; practical accomplishments, allegedly sprouting from socialist intentions, in fact distorted their genuine meaning. The abolition of the property bases of exploitation turned into providing a cheap infrastructure for private enterprise, into shifting the burden of keeping private enterprise alive on to the shoulders of the people, into 'socialisation of losses'. And so on.

But there is, in fact, a continuity within change and a change within continuity, in the content of the socialist utopia as much as in the direction of the practice it may inspire and inform. And it can hardly be otherwise considering the nature of socialism as a counter-culture, growing continually from contradictions and incongruences in the existing society. As society changes, as it sheds some of its flaws only to engender new ones, it is only natural that its counter-culture will rearrange its emphases. Rather than putting forth new branches on the old stem the socialist counter-culture tends to thrust out new shoots from the same imperishable root of criticism. This growth habit puts on the agenda, time and again, the task of reassessment of past traditions and of articulating anew the substance of continuity, even if for a brief spell the enormity of change tends to conceal the unbroken affinity. We will try now to take a provisional, certainly incomplete, stock of the elements of both.

First, let us see what modern criticism, however unprecedented, has in common with the counter-culture of capitalism historically formulated as the socialist project:

1. Above all, the conviction that whatever the solution to the problems of individual or collective sufferings, it is bound to be related, in a positive way, to the organisation of society as a whole. All socialist projects (this is perhaps the attribute which establishes the boundaries of the family of socialist ideas) are system-oriented. In this, they constitute an opposite of the bourgeois, individual-oriented culture.

The phrase 'in a positive way' in the above formulation ought to be stressed. In fact, no culture, including the bourgeois, can disregard entirely the existence of organisation on the societal level – be it an economic, political, or moral system – and declare its neutrality toward it. The typical attitude, however, taken throughout its history by the bourgeois culture, always boiled down to a negative postulate: let us get whatever constraints may arise from the societal organisation out of the way of the free individual. Societal power and coercion may be a necessity, but it is always a shackle. One can tolerate its presence and even seek its strengthening to safeguard the modicum of certainty and order in the individual's field of action, but one can hardly be enthused by this imperative, much less impute to it anything more than a sheer 'ground-clearing' function. Whatever happiness one may demand from life – whether enjoyment or dignity, self-actualisation or a clear conscience – can be obtained solely in conditions where the individual is master of his own action and free from constraints imposed by others. In C. B. Macpherson's admirable description of the fullest embodiment of bourgeois culture,' the philosophy of liberalism has been, from its origins in the seventeenth century, permeated by possessive individualism, which assumes that the individual is human *qua* proprietor of his own person, that the human essence is freedom from any but self-interested contractual relations with others, and that society is essentially a series of market relations between these free individuals'.[2] In practice, as de Tocqueville observed, in the conditions of privatised culture 'tyranny leaves the body free and directs its attack at the soul'.[3] Immanent critics of liberalism, who tended to locate further human emancipation in the realm of the spiritual, the moral, self-actualisation, were unable to look beyond the spellbound circle of the economic (bodily) liberty. Their self-actualisation recipes were often degenerated into not only encouraging the individual to find his fulfilment in the objects he subjects to his private mastery; but transforming the individual himself into such an object. As Horkheimer and Adorno put it, 'personality scarcely signifies anything more than shining white teeth and freedom from body odour and emotion'.[4]

The leitmotiv of the socialist counter-culture has always been, on the contrary, a positive attitude toward the societal whole. Society must be transformed, not in order to leave the individual alone, but to contribute actively to the fulness and wholesomeness of his life. The happy cohabitation of the individual and his society can be based, socialism insists, only on active cooperation and mutual complementation, never on real or illusory non-interference. One may say that socialism (like many a nationalist ideology) is community-oriented rather than society-oriented, in the sense of visualising the good society as a community, cemented by mutual aid and emotional dedication. The bourgeois culture privatises human happiness, the socialist counter-culture socialises it; it expounds individual fulfilment which is attainable in and through the society, rather than in spite of it.

Preoccupation with reform of the network of social relations in its totality remains the major point of contention between the socialist thought of today and the hegemonic bourgeois culture. It is brought into relief, first, in the critique of the present society. The misery of the individual is traced back to the flaws of the societal organisation. Diagnoses may differ, and they differ considerably if one surveys the whole field of socialist ideas, from the relatively traditional brand of socialist critique right up to the most radical extremes of 'total revolution'. But they all share the same tendency to aim at essential facets of the social system as such. The same individualism, which bourgeois culture worships and of which it is so proud, is here debunked. As Horkheimer wrote in 1947, 'the emancipation of the individual is not an emancipation from society, but the deliverance of society from atomisation, an atomisation which may reach its peak in periods of collectivisation and mass culture'.[5] The same bourgeois society, as Lelio Basso pointed out, which once aroused in man consciousness of his own individuality, today condemns him to desperation arising from solitude.[6] This solitude is forced upon the individual unsolicited, and is desperately, though vainly, resisted. To be sure, society supplies medicine with the poison, but the medicine is illusory while the poison is real; medicine, if anything, facilitates the poisonous action and effects. Men, in Stuart Hall's words, were 'forced, by the pressure from the consumer industries themselves, as they began to be providers of life and the givers of good things, to think of prosperity almost entirely in terms of things which they would purchase, possess, and enjoy as private individuals'.[7] The pursuit of salvation from solitude by the lonely individual only deepens the predicament from which he wishes to escape.

For the socialists of today the matter on the agenda is not just the alleviation of the plight of this or that group or class, not a relief to some specific, particular suffering of people who were left handicapped by a basically healthy and potent society. It is rather the matter of rescuing human society from the mortal danger of final decay to which the absurdities of late capitalism have brought it dangerously close. To quote Baran, 'in the earlier period the critical reaction was to the *injustice* of capitalism. It is only in relatively recent times when plenty is within easy reach and its attainment is obviously prevented by the continual dominance of capitalism that the *irrationality* of the system moves into the forefront of critical thought'.[8] And so – 'is not the case for the necessity and urgency of socialist transformation of the world of monopoly capital nothing but an exercise in rationalism?' Two conclusions follow from this totalistic view. First, according to the socialists of today, we have reached an 'all or nothing' situation. It is not possible any longer to improve, much less to cure, society in its present stage by a small change here and there, by doing away with one grievance today, another tomorrow. All the pains and miseries of all groups can and should be removed in one fell swoop, by the transformation of the entire society and its culture, or they will reappear again and again, even if temporarily patched up. Second, although the sufferings of various groups and classes are by no means equally intense and the shares of these classes in the total wretchedness of late capitalism do differ, there is no longer just one class anointed to raise the banner of the socialist transformation. Socialism is the solution for all, and neither its would-be enthusiasts nor its eventual enemies are necessarily class-ascribed. If there is a group cast by its social location into the role of a vanguard of socialism, it is most likely intellectuals (not conformist and faithful 'intellectual workers', who 'contract out' from the critical effort – C. P. Snow) who scan the totality of society from a broad historical perspective and therefore must inevitably come across proofs of its incurable absurdity. This was always, to be sure, the role ascribed to the intellectuals by the socialist utopia. But a century ago this role used to be reduced to the articulation of feelings of injustice and resentment which were already there, in the ranks of the proletariat, blatantly and unabashedly cast in the role of a pariah amidst the growing affluence of the privileged. Now, it is said, men must be rescued from their comatose acquiescence, from their endless race through the maze of privatised consumption, to realise the abominable misery of their situation as well as the need and feasibility of an alternative. They need intellectuals not just in the role of interpreters of their experience, but as the makers of experience which may lead to an alternative society via criticism of the *status quo*.

2. Egalitarianism has always been an unmistakably distinctive feature of the socialist utopia. Not only has it remained so, but its role in the totality of the socialist ideology is still on the increase; if for no other reason, then at least because it provides today one of the few remaining links between the utopia and the common-sense ruled by bourgeois culture. As Tom Bottomore observed, 'there is, as yet, no sign that in the western European countries the egalitarian impulse which came to life with the rise of the labour movement has lost its force'.[9] To be sure, this 'egalitarian impulse', by itself, does not necessarily lead to socialist conclusions. Late

capitalism has managed to accommodate this impulse and to translate it, under the aegis of accelerated economic growth, into a defused and harmless pursuit of a higher standard of living, which may, but does not necessarily, come into direct confrontation with the principle of unequal distribution. There are ample signs that what has been mistaken for 'egalitarian impulse' contains as much resentment of one's own disprivilege as of equality of those yet more deprived.

The way to a marriage with socialism will be, as contemporary socialists see it, long and rough. 'To fight against the exploitation of work', writes André Gorz, 'is necessarily also to fight against the ends for which labour is exploited.' But this is a theoretical statement, backed by a refined and sophisticated analysis of the productive mechanism of modern society and its logic of domination. Knowledge like this is not attainable directly from daily experience; it is not 'given' to the man in the street in his daily routine. In practice, as Gorz bitterly admits, 'wage claims are much more frequently motivated by rebellion against working conditions than by a revolt against the economic burden of exploitation borne by labour. They express a demand for as much money as possible to pay for the life wasted, the time lost, the freedom alienated in working under these conditions. . . . In short, the worker – even the highly-paid worker – tries to sell himself as dearly as possible because he cannot avoid *having* to sell himself'.[10] The egalitarian impulse, if redirected toward the pursuit of more money, far from opening men's eyes to the socialist alternative, blinds them to the societal, organic roots of their misery. In O'Connor's words, workers just 'cannot understand why higher wages and income and the accumulation of more material objects do not make them happy, but instead more dissatisfied. They do not understand that they are workers producing not only the objects they buy to satisfy their needs, but they are also producing the needs that the objects satisfy.'[11] So once again the task consists in breaking through the vicious circle of self-perpetuating processes. And this can be achieved only by stepping beyond the circle itself, attacking not the way in which capitalism works, but capitalism as such, whatever its performance as measured by day-to-day standards.

3. Thus, as before, the moral postulate of equality leads to an analytical assessment of the mechanism of alienation, which simul-

taneously perpetuates and is perpetuated by the capitalist ownership system, and to the strategic prescription to abolish capitalist
power. Alienation is at the root of inequality. It is not possible,
therefore, to settle the issue of equality in any real and conclusive
way unless the process of dis-alienation takes off in a genuine and
powerful manner. Alienation means depriving large masses of
people of all means of controlling their own lives. Private ownership is one of the most conspicuous sedimentations and instruments
of alienation, but not the only one. And so the abolition of private
property has lost, in the minds of contemporary socialists, much
of the magic power previously imputed to it. It is still accorded
a respectable place on the list of socialist priorities, but somewhat
qualified by the growing awareness that substitution of a state-
managed board for a private company will change little, if anything at all. The smug simplicity of earlier socialists, convinced
that universal happiness and freedom would descend automatically
on a world cleansed of private property, has given place to the
sobering awareness of the immensity of the tasks at hand. Tom
Bottomore has cogently expressed this new knowledge:

> It is no longer a question, in the industrial countries, of simply
> transforming the property system, of abolishing the private owner-
> ship of large-scale industry and eliminating the social class
> differences based upon great inequalities of wealth and income.
> There is also a need to change, in just as radical a fashion, the
> uses of technology, the organisation of work, the division of
> labour, and the system of authority in business enterprises; to
> devise new uses of leisure time, which might include the develop-
> ment of arts and crafts as secondary occupations capable of
> supplementing the mass production of essential goods by the
> creation of individual objects of beauty; and to encourage far
> larger numbers of people to take an active part in the manage-
> ment of public affairs, not only in industry, but in voluntary
> organisations of all kinds, and in local and regional communities.
> In seeking to achieve these ends socialist humanism should be
> guided by a moral ideal – which was that of the early socialists –
> namely, the conception of a community of creative, equal, and
> self-governing individuals, on a world scale. . . . Our hopes must
> lie in the greater rationality, self-control, and sense of responsi-
> bility, which equal opportunities to participate in the government
> of society should bring about.[12]

The emphasis more and more often falls on the last tenet: direct and effective participation in the actual governing. Gloomy experiences of nationalised serfdom have awakened the current generation of socialists to previously unsuspected aspects of equality. It has become increasingly clear that equality interpreted negatively promises little joy, and guarantees even less as a means of eradicating the roots of human bondage. That is, unless it is supplemented by positive equality, which manifests itself in the self-government of free individuals. In other words, equality is not a worthy goal unless inextricably coupled with freedom (and, as we have seen before, vice versa). This generation has learnt the painful way, while watching with growing dismay the convolutions of Soviet history, how the abolition of private property turned into the collectivisation of slavery. No wonder it looks with terror and alarm at the younger generation still, which has learnt nothing, remembers still less, and with a naïvety fed by ignorance declares freedom a bourgeois expedient to divert people from equality. If any lesson can be drawn from history, it is surely the absurdity of the supposition that freedom will spring all by itself from equality, and that therefore the right strategy for socialism is 'equality first, freedom later'. If it is true that the union of freedom and equality is not the easiest of marriages, it is none the less true that no equality remotely answering this name is possible if *not* married with freedom. As Svetozar Stojanović has soberly summed up the historical wisdom of his generation, 'the less socialism there was in practice, the more "liberalism" came to be regarded as a dirty word'.[13]

Once again, this new, or at least enhanced, understanding of equality and its place in the totality of the socialist utopia, confronts the present generation of socialist thinkers with an unexplored land and untried strategies. As might be expected, they attempt to escape the ensuing uncertainty by attaching their utopias to tangible, though incipient, solutions. The Yugoslav system seemed to many tailored to their needs. Roger Garaudy, the disenchanted orthodox communist, was among the most enthusiastic, in company with many a Polish, Hungarian, Czech and, perhaps, Russian reformer. In a way that is much less tied up with Yugoslav reality than he suspects, Garaudy advises the architect of future socialism systems:

The orientation of production becomes a function not of profit but of the needs of society, and this distinguishes all forms of socialism. But, contrary to practice in the statist, centralist (Soviet) model, these needs will not be determined from 'above' through central directives by the State and Party, but by the action of the market and of the demands which it discloses.[14]

Easy as it seems to have the market taking care of the 'needs of society', the picture prompts feelings curiously short of enthusiasm among those who have tried its wonders in practice. Wise after the fact, Stojanović entertains no illusions as to the socialist virtues of the market. The 'group-particularistic self-government', as he styles the Yugoslav system, will inevitably reinforce the power of the state, forced to act as referee among the muddle of selfish groups, and will massively generate the same well known *homo duplex* – 'the egoistic individual and group on the one hand, and the abstract citizen on the other'.[15] Stojanović's own suggestion is a 'personalist socialism', in which each individual is practically, concretely, actually engaged in the 'management of social tasks and in the definition of social interests'.[16] The suggestion, attractive as it may be, smells strongly of utopia. It *is* utopian, and Stojanović, as well as the whole of the *Praxis* group for which he speaks, admits it freely and unceremoniously. But then socialism climbs the heights of its power and influence when it supplies the utopia which expands the horizons of reality and thus creatively directs the making of human history.

The two tenets discussed above constitute the backbone of the socialist tradition of thought. Their presence has accomplished a great deal, and it is difficult to imagine the shape of modern society without the ubiquitous intellectual pressure of socialist ideas. Yet however impressive the accomplishments, they have still fallen far short of the stated targets. Hence the continuing utopian nature of the socialist project. On the other hand, quite a few avenues to which utopian hopes were originally bound have been explored in the process and successively abandoned. Historical experience does not crystallise only in the shape of reality; it sediments in its utopian conscience as well. And so there is change alongside continuity. The socialist utopia of the late twentieth century differs, in a number of significant respects, from its earlier versions.

1.   First and foremost, socialism is coming to be seen as, above all, the elimination of what is variously called 'surplus repression',

'over-repression', or 'superfluous dominance'. After long years of wandering, socialism is right back at the starting-point of the young Marx: socialist thinking consists once again today in developing the theory of dis-alienation.

Henri Lefebvre produced what is perhaps the fullest exposition of this idea:

> We may define an over-repressive society as one that, in order to avoid overt conflicts, adopts a language and an attitude dissociated from conflicts, one that deadens or even annuls opposition; its outcome and materialisation would be a certain type of (liberal) democracy where compulsions are neither perceived nor experienced as such; either they are recognised and justified, or they are explained away as the necessary conditions of (inner) freedom.[17]

The 'grand repression' of the great class battles, one may say, gave way to a plethora of minute, inconspicuous, repressive devices sprinkled generously over the entire field of everyday life. These seemingly innocuous devices, built into the consumer-defined life-world, into the mass culture, which continually absorbs and truncates new experience to the commonsensical formula of yesterday, and into every other area of the human life-process – securely guard the routine monotony of human conduct and disguise obedience as rationality. Pierre Boulez has pointed out that culture consists of transforming the improbable into the inevitable. This remarkably perceptive statement needs to be supplemented: the dominant culture consists of transforming everything which is not inevitable into the improbable. We may rephrase Lefebvre's definition while preserving its intention by saying that an over-repressive society is one which effectively eliminates alternatives to itself, and thereby relinquishes spectacular, dramatised displays of its power.

The cultural revolution, which alone can pave the way to the establishment of socialist human relations, can take place therefore only by the removal of the entire 'surplus repression' whose sole function is to sustain the historically transient form of domination. Conversely, the removal of such repression would be tantamount to a veritable cultural revolution of a socialist nature.

The issue of domination, which has always occupied a prominent place in the socialist project and critique, has been transplanted, in a sense, from the political to the cultural field. Though it may not be true that socialist thinkers now pay less heed to the key position held by the state, as the source of organised and legitimised violence, in the total structure of domination, they attach much less hope than in the past to the emancipating role of the capture of state power. More and more often one encounters the view that it is not a specific historical form of domination, but domination as such, which carries an essentially anti-socialist edge. The Soviet tyranny is not socialist simply because large-scale private ownership is absent. Outside the sphere of institutionalised party incarnations of socialism the belief is growing that, important as the eviction of bourgeois property may be, it is certainly not the key which opens the door leading directly to the gardens of socialism.

2.   The broadening of the socialist critique to attack the socio-cultural bases of domination and to reach its core, tougher and more resistant than any of its particular historic forms, is just one expression of the overall tendency to 'go to the roots' of alienation. The tendency is pronounced, expectedly, mainly inside 'intellectual socialism', which operates on the margins and frequently finds itself at loggerheads with organised political socialism. There is more than one reason for this intellectual tendency. There has been the frustrating experience of the Russian revolution; a growing realisation that the workers in the affluent West are unlikely, short of a major collapse of the system, to rally under the banner of a radical social transformation; the unabashed concubinage of socialism with narrow-minded and truculent nationalism; the keenness with which workers of many countries offered their enthusiastic support to totalitarian movements and their chauvinistic, genocidal ideologies; and, quite recently, a disgust with the present society and a disbelief in its capacity for improvement resulting in massive outbursts of irrationalism, mysticism, political infantilism, and cultural escapism. All this transcends the misdeeds, however grave, of private ownership alone, and calls for a wider analysis, digging deep into the foundations of modern society, on which both the bourgeois culture and its socialist counter-culture were originally erected.

Though the tendency may well be traced back deep into the past of the socialist utopia, it was the twin disasters of the German *populus* celebrating the advent of its new Dark Age and the blatant display of the Stalinist terror which really set it afloat. To these disasters Horkheimer and Adorno turned, trying to explain the reasons which prompted them to re-assess the Enlightenment, this fertile soil on which the socialist and bourgeois flowers grew side by side. It was nothing less than the Enlightenment itself, this universally acclaimed triumph of reason over mysticism and prejudice, which, in their view, injected into the hearts of modern men the incapacitating fear of 'departing from the facts'. Enlightenment is in its core 'mythic fear turned radical'. It equates freedom from fear with the elimination of anything unknown; and so the twin strategies it commends are either the naming and categorising which pass for intellectual mastery or the suppression and denial of everything extant which has escaped classification. Positivism, this commonsense of modern society, is perhaps the fullest and most faithful embodiment of the spirit of Enlightenment; but 'the pure immanence of positivism, its ultimate product, is no more than a so to speak universal taboo. Nothing at all may remain outside, because the mere idea of outsideness is the very source of fear'.[18] Positivism means, therefore, a most brutal suppression of alternative modes of existence, as well as of all attempts to redeem the unrealised hopes of the past. But accepting the 'facts' as the only safe haven of tranquillity and freedom from fear means neither more nor less than accepting the dominant conventions of science, commerce and politics. The two pressures built into modern man's life-world reinforce each other, transforming political dissent into an attack upon reason, and any 'departure from the facts' into political dynamite.

This false security is, however, fraught with dangerous traps, and so the Enlightenment carries the seeds of its own violent destruction. Infected with *horror vacui*, but allowed to enjoy his terror-free existence only if he accepts a rationality cut down to the size of the dominant social institutions, the denizen of the post-Enlightenment world is, if he rebels, abandoned to paranoia. Hence the fascist tumours are natural outgrowths of the Enlightenment rather than its denial:

> The true benefit for the *Volksgenosse* lies in collective approval of his anger. . . . It is a luxury for the masses. . . . The paranoiac forms of consciousness tend toward the formation of alliances, parties, and rackets. Their members are afraid of believing in their delusions on their own. Projecting their madness, they see conspiracy and proselytism everywhere. The established group always adopts a paranoiac attitude to others. . . .[19]

One would expect that the paranoiac propensities bred by modern society would pollute any attempts at self-emancipation from its shackles. It is likely that such attempts will be misdirected and transmogrified into equally paranoiac mass hysteria or futile individual escapism. The foreboding that this will be the case prompted Horkheimer and Adorno themselves to withdraw, at a later stage, from direct topical commitment into the safe seclusion of highly sophisticated and correspondingly esoteric philosophical ratiocinations.

The sense of isolation and solitude haunting the radical critics of late capitalism has been aptly expressed by Marcuse:

> To the degree to which liberation presupposes the development of a radically different consciousness (a veritable counter-consciousness) capable of breaking through the fetishism of the consumer society, it presupposes a knowledge and sensibility which the established order, through its class system of education, blocks for the majority of the people. . . . The isolation of the New Left is thus well founded. . . . Allergic to its factual separation from the masses . . . the movement displays inferiority complexes, defeatism, and apathy.[20]

It is only too easy to indulge, on the one hand, in the high-flown sophistry which will be safely protected from pollution only because largely irrelevant to ordinary human experience and uncommunicative to the man in the street. On the other hand, insufficiently theoretically informed but impetuous and impulsive action may well deprive individual rebellion of its universal, culture-creative potential. 'The standardised use of "pig language", the petty-bourgeois anal eroticism, the use of garbage as a weapon against helpless individuals, these are manifestations of a pubertarian revolt against the wrong target.'[21] And so the pursuit of the socialist utopia leads today, as it always did, between the Scylla of domesticated 'progressivism' and the Charybdis of uncontrolled and precocious outbursts of anger, declining into short-lived histrionics, individual withdrawals or politically disguised criminality.

3. If many versions of traditional socialism tended to emphasise 'socialisation of happiness' to the detriment of personality and subjectivity, the radical extensions of the socialist utopia of today put human consciousness and subjectivity in the very centre of their revolutionary project. This is precisely what one might expect

in the light of previous considerations. The crucial role of sub-jectivity in the process of emancipation is indeed a logical conclusion if emancipation has been defined in terms of the removal of 'surplus domination' and the renascence of Reason. The logical chain is well depicted by Karl Klare:

> The New Left stresses that the locus of revolutionary social change is not limited to major political and economic institutions but extends to the consciousness of daily life of the individual. Consciousness is seen as the bearer of the social, economic, sexual, cultural, ideological, and common-sense under-pinnings that form the moral basis of the old way of life and old insti-tutions. Accordingly, it must be radically and totally altered along with the structure of society in order to create the normative and intersubjective basis of the new way of life. . . . Cultural revolu-tion and the critique-in-action of everyday life are therefore at the core of the revolutionary process from the outset.[22]

Transformed consciousness is both the necessary condition and the essence of the passage to socialism. It is not enough that the structure of domination be changed on the societal level, well above the heads, and the daily practice, of ordinary men and women; it is their own world perception, its depth and sensitivity, the way they interact with their immediate and indirect environment, the way they control it and mould their entire style of life which must be altered, so we are told, for socialism to come to pass.

This shift of emphasis, again, may be attributed to many causes. One is the intellectual impact of phenomenology and existentialism, which have left their imprint on the totality of modern philosophical anthropology, the socialist utopia being, naturally, no exception. Today one cannot discuss human emancipation or the human predicament in general without expounding a theory of the life-world and intentional grounds of meaning. In our view of the human condition emancipation has become well-nigh coterminous with the freedom for self-actualisation, and serfdom with the shackles imposed by the 'natural attitude' of the world, whose mental images gained an independent life and took on the appearance of an outer, indomitable reality. The process of emancipation tends to appear therefore as the debunking of such a 'natural attitude', or common-sense, or naïve world view, or placid acceptance of everyday con-structs and meanings produced by others. In this sense, many a socialist statement of today shares its language and its concerns with the rest of currently fashionable brands of philosophical anthropology.

But another reason for the shift deserves particular attention. I discussed earlier the increasingly intellectual-elitist status of the more radical offshoots of the contemporary socialist utopia. It is elitist in a double sense. First, it is practically confined to the ultra-developed fringe of the modern world; and within this affluent suburb of the globe it is still further expropriated by the thin stratum of the educated middle class. The links of this stratum with the actual victims of whatever injustice and exploitation the modern society may be guilty of (again in the same double sense) is, to say the least, tenuous. The virtual absence of such links permits the producers of utopia to spread their wings and to fly high as never before; but from the heights of 'total radicalism' the daily concerns and troubles of the common man become barely discernible, and the yearnings which have brought the critical spirit to celestial regions can easily pass for the universal pinings of the universal man.

The conversion of the philosophical self-awareness of the age (with the socialist utopia following suit) from 'hard' to 'soft' factors, from the image of the tough reality 'over there' to subjective consciousness, from objective constraints to the distortion of language, from restructuring society to the individual's refusal to be structured by the society, reflect, in a sense, the growing emancipation of the intellectual elite as a whole from the turmoils of common life, and their increasing detachment from the trivial, banausic preoccupations visible on the level of survival. It is easy, in the circumstances, to view the group's privileged position as a foothold maintained on behalf of mankind in the world of the future, and while confessing privately experienced spiritual tormentings, to enlighten, patronisingly, the incredulous man-in-the-street: *De te fabula narratur.*

Thus a privilege accorded by affluent society is misread as liberation from the thraldom of bourgeois morality. If Marx was such a keen advocate of the work ethic, as we are told, it was because he failed to sneak out of the cultural-psychological grip of capitalism. But we, as it were, have arrived at the 'post-accumulation era' (Klare) and so have little use for the work ethic. More than that, 'the reified and alienated social relations characteristic of societies in which the mass of people are permanently caught up in the struggle for survival, need no longer determine the quality of human interaction, culture, and sexuality'.[23] One is left to wonder what does determine the culture and sexuality of these masses of people who, in defiance of the post-accumulation boredom of their spiritual vanguard, stubbornly insist on being still caught up in the struggle for survival, and to ask whether these sceptical masses will see how the relaxation of sexual codes will make their struggle easier. They will perhaps agree with Marcuse that any socialist society worth the name ought to be 'light, pretty, playful', but will they consider the Orphic spirit of the intellectual elite as the first glimpse into their own socialist future? Would they recognise the fighters for their cause in students releasing their Oedipus complexes by hurling bottles at their professors? Would they identify with 'rich man's socialism'?

But if the 'subjectivity-oriented' radicals tend to play down, if not neglect altogether, the real hardships of their 'own' poor and handicapped, the neglect is even more astounding and even less guilt-ridden so far as the poor on the world scale are concerned. As Deutscher wrote in 1967, 'the concept of the elite as the main agent of socialism appeals to you because you think it frees you from the need to analyse the economic and class structure of society. It envelops the whole big mountain in a fog, with the peak – the elite – sticking out clearly for you to see'.[24] But it is a two-tier fog; it frees one from the need to analyse the structure of the world as well. The thesis of the 'post-accumulation' era becomes a monstrous travesty when cast against the backcloth of the famished earth. Whatever the motives, the 'post-accumulation' preoccupations of the new radicals are in tune with the vernacular ethnocentrism of an affluent society's cultural idiom. It is within this idiom that Daniel Bell wrote his 'venture in social forecasting' under the pretentious title *The Coming of Post-Industrial Society*, and proceeded to page 483 without mentioning that the wonders of the American somersault into the benign House of Solomon have been performed in a hunger-stricken world, bringing the so-called Third World into the story only as the 'international context', the 'outer [!] limit of our trajectory'.[25] It is within the same idiom, though in a somewhat perverse way, that the new radicalism operates, oblivious of the painful gap between the post-accumulation of the few and the pre-accumulation of the multitude. What such radicals risk, in their luxurious version of the socialist utopia, is a reinforcement of the same vernacular ethnocentrism, which, as Deutcher warned, is an anti-socialist force by definition.

E

To make the risk graver still, it has its roots in the shape of the challenge the heirs of the socialist utopia face in our phase of history. Since its birth, the status of the socialist project has undergone a fateful change; it can no longer claim an unqualified utopian status. Notwithstanding the contempt in which they are held by the scientific age, projects which legitimately carry the utopian name do enjoy enviable advantages; claiming a location in the future, they can credibly ignore, as inconclusive, the evidence of the past. Themselves an object of scientific contempt, they can view with righteous disbelief and derision the 'crawling realism' of scientific objections. Science and utopia operate, so to speak, in separate regions of the universe; their assertions are subject therefore to the rules of separate (even autonomous) epistemologies, and neither bind nor qualify each other with any authority other than ideological. Hence the imaginative freedom enjoyed by utopias, and their power to supply alternative pivots of social action. The socialist project of the late twentieth century can claim neither this freedom nor that power. In this sense, it has lost a good deal of its utopian status. Quite a few areas of social reality have been shaped in its name, and have even appropriated the name itself. Utopia and reality are no longer sovereign lands, with socialism coming down unequivocally on one side of the border. Claiming still an unimpaired utopian vision, socialism has awakened somewhat abruptly to the fact that it is now exposed to empirical scrutiny and argument. The utopian function of the socialist project can be retained, in the circumstances, only on condition that its critical edge is directed against *all* reality. Since this reality encompasses sectors styled as socialist, socialist *utopia* must take a critical stance toward socialist *reality* as well as capitalist reality.

It seems that the single most important change in the social situation of the socialist project is that it can no longer preserve its character as the utopian *spiritus movens* of history, whilst remaining the counter-culture of capitalism alone. Hence, such changes as become prominent in contemporary socialist thinking derive their inspiration and force from the critique of *both* the major established systems of modern society. Here again the socialist utopia has come full circle. It began as an audacious challenge levelled by Reason and Justice against an order founded on irrationality and avarice. With the socialist idea taking root in political practice Reason was slowly objectivised as the 'law of history' or 'historical necessity'; irrationality materialised as planless, competitive management by the rich; justice was defined as redistribution of wealth, and avarice as economic exploitation. The ascent of socialism came to be seen as a majestic act of Nature, unveiling its future stages, already present as an inexpugnable potential. Whether this would take place as a gradual, self-propelling process, or as a dramatic excavation of the nugget of the future from beneath the slag of the past, was a relatively minor matter, however vehement the argument it aroused. The historical drama was seen by the advocates of both views alike as a play staged 'over there', in a supra-human social reality, and following a scenario irrevocably fixed by history. The content of the drama was the wrestle between the young and the old. Everybody knows that the young is weaker at first, but everybody knows as well that he will inevitably grow in strength, while his adversary will not – and that he will eventually be enthroned by Nature even if he does nothing at all to bring his triumph about. Socialism was the young social system, capitalism was the old one. The outcome of *battles* between the two might hinge on human dedication and acumen; but the result of the *war* was already settled in advance by the law of history.

This view of the historical drama of socialism as a war between two social *systems*, of military operations waged by supra-human commanders-in-chief, with results known in advance, is by no means a matter of the past. It is still firmly entrenched in institutionalised sediments of socialism's stormy invasion of the political scene. But a new tendency is gaining ground, and it is not by chance that it looks for inspiration to the young Marx and to Hegel's legacy. With its advance the socialist utopia returns to square one; to the idea of an audacious and heroic *tour-de-force*, pitted against all odds and counting on nothing but its own inner resources of human courage and imagination. As Kołakowski has recently put it: 'from a world given in all its details, accomplished, determined in its evolutionary development and accessible for either a description, which puts on record its attributes while minimising all interference, or for exploitation, which is incapable of altering the evolutionary course of the whole, we have passed to a world, which from the start and in each of its stages, we have to admit as our own co-product'.[26] Hence, at least in part, the new focus on the individual, now seen as the major and decisive battlefield. Increasingly, the drama is seen not as a struggle between socialism and capitalism (two consecutive systems of social organisation), but between socialism and commonsense (two alternative ways of tackling the human condition). The conclusion that the fate of the battle, and the responsibility for it, falls on the shoulders of each and every individual, follows almost by itself. The dream of a rationally organised community (which bourgeois culture and its traditional socialist counter-culture hailed in unison) begins to be viewed with suspicion, as a contrivance to release men and women from the self-control and responsibility which render them human; and as a project which derives its attraction only from the experience of modern civilisation which offers individuality as solitude, individual responsibility as abandonment, and self-control as a series of inescapable frustrations. Deprived in this way of their individuality, men and women eagerly lend their ears to the promises of the monotonous predictability of the rationally programmed society, which, upon closer scrutiny, turns out to be a recipe for totalitarianism. Commonsense is, indeed, an escape from freedom; but to look for this sort of retreat, men had first to be forced into a situation in which freedom is available only in conjunction with terror or impotence. We have now enough historical evidence to suspect that such situation is generated by capitalist conditions with no more intensity than it is by the traditional socialist treatment of their ills.

9

Roads from Utopia

Commonsense contains few, if any, proofs that socialism is 'inevitable' or, indeed, feasible. Commonsense, as Ernst Bloch pointed out, is founded on the assumption that the form of life people experience will last indefinitely, that 'men will always be men'. Now the feasibility of the socialist project hinges precisely on the hope that men may, given the right conditions, cease to be as we know them and as we seem always to have known them. To this hope, however, the sobering popular wisdom of endlessly duplicated individual and collective 'practical lessons' is opposed.

The structural-functionalist theory of society assumed that whatever 'spiritual' or cultural integration of a social system takes place must be based on 'consensus', that is, on the favourable attitude taken by the bulk of the population to fundamental values on which the entire structure of a given society rests. The remarkable thing about the critics of functionalism is that they tended to agree, if only tacitly, with this crucial assumption. Often this led them to expounding opposite, though equally dogmatic and one-sided, descriptions of the existing society. In so far as they denied (for one reason or another) that a decisive majority of the members of society 'love', or 'like', or 'enthusiastically surrender to' the existing system, they could explain the system's visible strength and invulnerability only by referring to non-cultural means of 'integration', and chiefly to economic and political compulsion. Thus both adversaries, having identified culture with values and evaluation, condemned themselves to the dilemma of 'consensus' versus 'coercion', as the two alternative but equally unsatisfactory and partial explanations of systemic continuity. In fact a strong model of the system can be erected on neither of these two poles of the analytically false continuum, nor in its middle. A most important contribution of Frank Parkin's outstanding study[1] consists in dissociating, *de facto*, the problem of cultural integration of the system from the very different problem of the acceptance, or sympathetic acceptance, of the structural principles of the whole edifice. According to Parkin, the 'dominant' value system, diffused and sponsored by the major institutional order (which is always the order of a specific class dominance) is actively assisted in its cultural-integrative action by a 'subordinate value system' which, even if far from committing itself to the defence of the system, and farther still from inspiring, or being inspired by, sympathy for the system, still upholds it actively by promoting 'accommodative responses to the facts of inequality and low status'. This is precisely what Gramsci depicted, though not in so many words, as the 'vertical' structure of civil society, in which the ruling philosophical formula is linked to the commonsensical level on which the rules of individual accommodation to the societally produced predicament are supplied.

The subordinate value system is, so to speak, a perverse reflection of the dominant system of ideas in a number of senses: not only for the success of the dominant idiom in belittling the feasibility of alternative realities, not only for its achievements in substituting 'Nature' where one should read 'history', but also for the fact that the dominant idiom promotes 'individuation' of sufferings, and so excludes the generalisation of resentment or, rather, wards off the transformation of misery into dissent. The conditions to which working-class communities are exposed, Parkin observes, 'generate a meaning-system which is of purely parochial significance, representing a design for living based upon localised social knowledge and face-to-face relationships'. As to the 'radical value system', one which promotes 'an oppositional interpretation of social inequalities', it (here Parkin reiterates the traditional Marxian view) has no roots in 'spontaneously' developing commonsense. It is a party, a politically institutionalised attitude, which provides the foundation of a radical value system. In Parkin's view, one can say, the class consciousness of the dispossessed is inevitably, and by definition, a politically institutionalised consciousness. Without such a level of institutionalisation the dispossessed remain in the grip of the subordinate meaning system: 'it is reasonable to regard trade unionism and instrumental collectivism generally as an accommodative response to inequality'.[2]

Two further comments, however, seem in order. First, for inequality (as distinct from such misery as approaches the level of subsistence or falls below it) to be a motive for action, either accommodative or oppositional, a postulate of equality must first take root in the popular mind as a cultural norm. There was not such a norm in the medieval type of corporate society, in which the style of life proper to one's station was the order of the day. The postulate of equality was first established in culture by the bourgeois class. Having grown out of the bourgeois culture, the radical meaning system, phrased in terms of inequality and its transcendence, retains the birth mark of the parent culture. However critical of its ancestor, it communicates with him easily, being articulated in basically identical language. It can, therefore, be 'assimilated' in one way or another by the parent culture, thus passing from the 'radical' to the 'subordinate' category. In Irving Howe's words, 'what occurs characteristically during the growth of the welfare state is a series of "invasions", by previously neglected or newly cohered social groups demanding for themselves a more equitable portion of the social product and appealing to the common ideology of welfarism as the rationale of their demands'.[8] And so the line between the radical and the subordinate is by no means tight and drawn forever. The existence of a subordinate meaning system sustains the possible emergence of a radical one if the dominant system fails to keep its promise to accommodate demands made in the name of equality; and vice versa. The radical meaning system, as described by Parkin, does not necessarily act as an outward-pointing force. It can still play a supporting role, rescuing the system from collapse and in some indirect way contributing to the integration of the whole.

Second, even with the postulate of equality firmly established in culture, what is noticed and recorded as manifestations of inequality may vary. Human beings are dissimilar in many different respects, but only relatively few dissimilarities are culturally classified as belonging to the set of attributes which can and ought to be assessed in terms of inequality and so release an egalitarian thrust. The postulate of equality is most commonly applied to one field only: the distribution and redistribution of possessions. Such redistributive equality can therefore trigger off and guide human action only in conditions of private ownership; it is tied up with the institution of property as defined by bourgeois culture. It is necessarily oriented toward the past and aimed at correcting structures already fixed. The postulate cannot reach, neither can it guide human action, beyond that. Its power, as well as its weakness, reflect the fact that while the consciousness that other people get more from their life is on the whole unpleasant, there is little pleasure in the thought that nobody is better off than oneself. Rational action based on the postulate of distributive equality will consist of summoning such force as is available to enhance a group's position in the context of inequality. And so the experience of relative deprivation, as mediated by the norm of distributive equality, leads in no direct, logical way to the opposition to inequality as such. People seem to need deprivation of others to measure their own 'emancipation'.

In the light of the above considerations, it seems that the advocates of socialism who expect that, left to themselves, in 'natural conditions', the relatively deprived will inevitably turn into fighters against class society as such, commit the error of *petitio principi*. It is widely assumed that the flagrantly unequal share of workers in the national wealth (according to John Westergaard's estimate as little as 1 per cent of the British population holds as much as 41 per cent of the entire property[4]) contains the necessity, or almost necessity, of working-class radicalism. If the expectation fails to come true it is perceived as a puzzling event which requires an explanation; some powerful adverse factors must have been at work, to *prevent* workers from becoming radical. The adverse factors usually fall into one, or both, of two categories: the indolence of socialist intellectuals and/or politicians who failed to 'present a policy of direct attack upon the established structure of power and property'; and the 'ideological lies' of the ruling class which misled the workers into believing that the existing structure was, or might become, advantageous to them. Whatever the explanation given, the common assumption is that it is the *lack* of radical opposition, rather than its presence, which requires explanation.

Others accept that the abundant and ever-growing evidence makes a revision of theory imperative and unavoidable. Hence attempts to build a new theory which would show the informed radicalism of the deprived, particularly of the working class, as an exceptional phenomenon which requires an unusual concatenation of non-inevitable, perhaps contingent events, to occur (Althusser's 'over-determination' belongs here) and to be explained. What the desired theory is to show is, in the first place, that the developments which were previously considered a disaster or 'betrayal', resulting from collusion or criminal neglect, are in fact what is to be expected in the present stage of late industrial development. And so the

Socialist Scholars' Conference in the USA considered and approved
Martin Nicolaus's view that 'the probability of a working-class
revolution varies inversely with the rate of exploitation. The higher
the rate of exploitation, the bigger the margin of surplus controlled
by the capitalist class. The bigger the margin, the more easily can
labour demands be satisfied'.[5] Two years earlier Perry Anderson
pointed out that 'a purely working-class party tends, by its very
nature, towards either corporatism or outright subordination'.[6] And
André Gorz attempted to elucidate the actual social mechanism
of this subordination:

> Workers endorse the employers' power every day, by clocking
> in on time, by submitting to work which they have no hand in
> organising, by taking home pay-packets. . . . Modern industry's
> dominant tendency is no longer the maximum exploitation of the
> workers. . . . The dominant tendency is to 'integrate' the workers
> into the system. . . . Regularity is what matters most'.[7]

On the whole, the proposed theories do not deny the presence of
exploitation but they deny, or question, previous assumptions about
the causal link between exploitation and the tendency toward
socialism.

The problem is not new. The careful reader of *Capital* asks himself more than once how Marx actually envisaged the chain of
'inevitabilities' which connects the appropriation of surplus value
with a socialist revolution. The answers varied, but none withstood
a close scrutiny. Was it the notorious contradiction between productive forces and productive relations? If so, who would be the
agent of change: managers, legislators? Would there be a total
collapse of the system, similar to that which occurred in slave
society? Or would there be a revolt born of destitution and despair
which might bring down the system of exploitation? In the last
case – does not the mitigation of poverty cancel the prospect of
socialism? In fact, as I have hinted before, *Capital*, except for a
number of paragraphs which are clearly tacked on to the main
story, presents a cogent case for the self-perpetuation of exploitation. As a cohesive and systematic theory *Capital* distinguishes, as
inevitable developments (contrary to some of the author's outspoken
declarations and almost all institutionalised commentaries), the
continuous subordination of the workers to their rulers and to the
system as such, and the emergence of workers' defensive organisations cut to the measure of market relations and private property,

F

that is organisations which pursue redistributive aims. The one 'necessity' whose nature is far from clear is that which is supposed to lead to the socialist channelling of workers' disaffection.

Indeed, implying such a necessity would mean ascribing to Marx a radically deterministic image of man, clearly at odds with the Marxian 'philosophy of praxis'. It would imply that, for Marx, one can indeed derive men's spiritual contents from their material conditions; and, moreover, that these conditions are describable and 'knowable' in only one way. But both assumptions stand in downright opposition to the basic tenets of the Marxian theory of society (though not to its institutionalised interpretations). The most one can say about the determining role of material conditions is that they set limits to ideas which may be adequately used to account for them. It is the degree of adequacy, as Gramsci repeatedly stressed, which makes the popular adoption of some ideas more likely than that of the others. But invariably there is more than one set of ideas which may be satisfactorily attached to a volume of experience as 'making sense of it', as transforming the experienced into the intelligible and generating a moderately rational set of adaptive behavioural precepts. In the ensuing competition between ideas the socialist set is less likely than its rivals to get hold of human imagination; its 'proof' lies in the future, while there is little in past experience which may be presented as evidence pointing unambiguously to its plausibility. It is not contained in the experience itself, unlike other 'generalising' theories which can boast the support of a long series of known actions which did bring at least partial success and relief. A number of socialist thinkers, who have refused to give up the search for inevitability, attach their hopes to the notion of the dispossessed being 'forced' into accepting the socialist utopia by default; what is 'inevitable' is the bankruptcy of 'experience generalising' theories. The time will arrive sooner or later when capitalism will no longer be able to redeem its pledge. The hope is that the workers' struggle, still led by the logic of capitalist commonsense, will somehow inevitably transcend the forms in which it can still be squared with capitalist domination. What the adherents of such a view do not show, and are hardly able to show, is the way in which the 'inevitable' socialist nature of this 'beyond' is assured. On the basis of historical evidence, it appears that there is more than one way leading *from* capitalism, even if the hopes of 'inevitable transcendence' come true.

The thirst for inevitability, as Horkheimer and Adorno would say, is itself an unmistakable sign of the strength with which positivism, this self-consciousness of an alienated society, holds human imagination under its sway. The zeal with which the hunt for the 'missing link' is being carried on can be explained only by the fact that commonsense, overawed by an all-powerful reality, will bow only to an even more powerful and more 'real' reality; and only when confronted in this way will it loosen its iron grip sufficiently to release unconventional human action. Hence the amazing number of socialist thinkers who go out of their way to convince – mostly each other – that the implementation of socialist values is not only desirable, but inevitable as well. It seems that the reason of our age, whether conformist or critical, shuns situations of indeterminacy and tends to flee the terrifying void into the homely shelter of the necessary or customary. This 'craving for necessity' is the deepest and most indelible brand of alienation. Thus the belief that the transformation of socialist utopia into reality *must* take place is needed to inspire the energy and determination which is perhaps necessary for this belief to come true. A theoretical 'proof' of the inevitability of socialism will, of course, change nothing in the structure of reality. Its effect can be only of a psychological nature; it can prompt people, still in the grip of alienation, to embark on the daring venture of emancipation.

But can it really? It seems unlikely that the kind of emancipation and freedom the modern socialist thinkers dream of can be won with arms forged in the smithy of alienation. It is, on the contrary, the relinquishment of the powerful internalised urge to employ such arms which is the preliminary and paramount condition for this emancipation. If the advent of socialism involves the creation of a new culture, the cultural image under which the transition takes place is not an irrelevant issue; in fact, it may well be the decisive factor, on which the character of the succeeding system will depend. The proponents of the socialism of 'inevitability' will smile contemptuously at the memory of hopes that 'the strengthening of the state will bring nearer its demise', or that rampant terror will enhance human liberties; but they fail to see the ominous logical affinity between such hopes and their own. The idea that people will free themselves while acting as convinced agents of inevitability can only deepen and reinforce the mental grip of unfreedom. It certainly cannot bring a step nearer the new, emancipated culture which these thinkers see as the hub of socialism. If socialism is to be seen, as it claims, as a further inquiry into yet unexplored regions of human freedom, it can be brought about only in a free and unconstrained dialogue between all the actors of the historical process. We know of no example of people being forced into freedom; we know too many examples of people forced into slavery while they are told that they are being led to freedom.

Only such roads may lead to socialism as are cut from the same rock as the socialist utopia itself. One hopes that this rule would make distortions of the road embarked on under socialist auspices less likely. And for a generation which has witnessed Soviet totalitarianism, exotic socialisms of long knives, and student radicalism running wild and proud of its militant intolerance, such hope is not something to be dismissed lightly.

One more remark is in order. The utopias born of one reality are many, and often at variance with each other. They differ in audacity, in the distance of the horizons they draw, in the locus of the real world in which they place the leg of the trammel to draw the new horizon. New utopias rarely wait until their predecessors exhaust their creative power, much less until they materialise and leave the realm of utopia forever; one utopia treads on the heels of the other, thus forcing it into redeploying its arms and opening a second battle-line. It is only for a few brief moments that a utopia may enjoy the luxury of an unchallenged status and focus all its guns on the unique enemy, the condemned reality, which, in Trotsky's words, 'is only the present'. Drawing a new, more distant horizon not only exposes unsuspected facets of the already familiar reality, but creates a new 'beyond', which promptly takes over the seductive mysteriousness of the previous one, now incorporated into the field of 'established' vision. Sooner rather than later, this new 'beyond' will attract daring explorers who will draw new, ever more distant, horizons, and thus prepare the ground for a further round of intellectual exploration and adventures of the imagination.

To be fair, the attack does not catch the old utopia – now cast in the unenviable role of a disguised orthodoxy – off guard. Very early it will have fortified itself against all critique from a position yet more utopian and radical than the one it took originally. Having been excommunicated by the reigning culture as an insane and pitiful fantasy, it promptly draws its own frontier dividing 'true' realism from 'genuine' insanity and irresponsibility. It fights the barbarian cohorts sweeping across this new frontier with the same arms that were used by the dominant culture it challenged: it will charge them with adventurism, ignorance, reason-defying utopianism, voluntarism, and the full range of sins committed against science, law and order, the will of the majority, and the indomitable trends of history. This will, of course, lend credibility to the ultra-radical critique, and in its turn exacerbate the 'realistic' zealotry of the now-less-radical utopia, and *da capo*.

The modern socialist utopia fortified itself against the farther reaches of the 'beyond' at a relatively early stage of its history. It hastened to cut itself loose from ties with more radical brands of counter-culture. It came into its own precarious self-identity through fierce wars of liberation waged against all subjectivity-extolling, anti-institutional strands within the same anti-capitalist camp. It took Marx four-fifths of a German ideology to exorcise the ghost of Stirner; Marx kept his most poisonous arrows for his fellow heretics rather than the common orthodox enemy, and the brief though stormy history of the First International contributed more to establishing the outer limits of the permissible utopian project than to strengthening its case against capitalist reality. The socialist utopia placed itself at that time firmly in the role of a prospective culture of industrial society intended to replace the capitalist one. It rejected as utopian and irrealistic in their turn the projects which ventured beyond the vistas of scientism and industry, rational organisation and technology. As one would expect, however, neither the battle nor its momentary results proved to be final. The ultra-utopia was merely pushed aside, to bide its time and to claim eventually the status of the counter-culture of existing society, when that society's more universal features are exposed. The body of utopian criticism is bound to remain, as before, inherently fissiparous. Men climb, as it were, successive hills only to discover from their tops virgin territories which their never-appeased spirit of transcendence urges them to explore. Beyond each successive hill they hope to find peacefulness of the end. What they do find is the excitement of the beginning. Today as two thousand years ago, 'hope that is seen is not hope. For who hopes for what he sees?' (Paul to the Romans, 8.24).

Notes

CHAPTER 1

1 C. Wright Mills, *The Sociological Imagination* (New York, Oxford University Press, 1959), p. 190.
2 *Revue de métaphysique et de morale*, part XX, p. 119. Quoted by W. H. G. Armytage, *Yesterday's Tomorrows, A Historical Survey of Future Societies* (London, Routledge & Kegan Paul, 1968), p. 36.
3 Teilhard de Chardin, *The Future of Man* (London, Collins, 1964), p. 72.
4 Raymond Ruyer, *L'Utopie et les utopies* (Paris, Presse Universitaire de France, 1950), p. 17.
5 John Passmore, *The Perfectibility of Man* (London, Duckworth, 1972), p. 280.
6 Ruyer, op. cit., p. 13.
7 Virgilio Melchiore, 'La conscienza utopica', in *L'utopia nel mondo moderno* (Florence, Vallentri Editore, 1969), p. 88.
8 Joseph Gusfield, 'Economic Development as a Modern Utopia', in *Aware of Utopia*, ed. David W. Plath (Urbana, University of Illinois Press, 1971), p. 76.
9 Lewis Mumford, 'Utopia, The City and the Machine', *Daedalus*, vol. 94 (1965), p. 275. In a surprisingly similar vein Ruyer described the role of utopias: 'Les utopias sont comme des enveloppes de brume sous lesquelles s'avancent des idées neuves et réalisables' (op. cit., p. 115).
10 Frank E. Mannel, 'Toward a Psychological History of Utopias', *Daedalus*, vol. 94 (1965), p. 306.
11 Fred Charles Iklé, 'Can social predictions be evaluated?', *Daedalus*, vol. 96 (1967), p. 755.
12 Daniel Bell, 'The Year 2000 – The Trajectory of an Idea', *Daedalus*, vol. 96 (1967), p. 643.
13 François Bloch-Lainé, 'The Utility of Utopias for Reformers', *Daedalus*, vol. 94 (1965), p. 420.

CHAPTER 2

1 Cf. Chad Walsh, *From Utopia to Nightmare* (New York, Harper and Row, 1962), p. 40.
2 Francis Bacon, *Novum Organum*, I, 85, 92.
3 Marie Jean Nicholas Condorcet, *Esquisse d'un tableau historique des progrès de l'esprit humain* (1795). The English translation in *The Idea of Progress*, ed. George H. Hildebrandt (University of California Press, 1949), p. 337.

4 Chad Walsh, op. cit., p. 174.
5 Auguste Comte, *The Positive Philosophy*, trans. Harriet Martineau (London, Bell, 1896).
6 Richard Gerber, *Utopian Fantasy* (London, Routledge & Kegan Paul, 1955), p. 45.
7 William Barrett, *Irrational Man* (London, Heinemann, 1972), p. 204.
8 Alexis de Tocqueville, *The Old Regime* . . ., trans. Stuart Gilbert (New York, 1955), p. 140.
9 Cf. John Passmore, *The Perfectibility of Man* (London, Duckworths, 1972), p. 173.
10 Crane Brinton, 'Utopia and Democracy', *Daedalus*, vol. 94 (1965), p. 356.
11 H. Stuart Hughes, 'Mass Culture and Social Criticism', *Daedalus*, vol. 89 (1960), p. 388.
12 Raymond Ruyer, *L'Utopie et les utopies* (Paris, Presse Universitaire de France, 1950), p. 59.
13 Cf. *Lenin and Leninism*, ed. Bernard W. Eisenstadt (Lexington, Lexington Books, 1971).
14 Barrington Moore Jr, *Social Origins of Dictatorship and Democracy* (Harmondsworth, Penguin Books, 1966), p. 486.
15 Cf. Lewis Mumford, *The Story of Utopias* (New York, Boni & Liveright, 1922).
16 Chad Walsh, op. cit., pp. 63, 89.
17 This point has recently been convincingly discussed by Adam Ulam, 'Socialism and Utopia', *Daedalus*, vol. 94 (1965), pp. 391ff.
18 Ivan Illich, 'Maintaining a Wattage Threshold', *New York Times*, 17 September 1973.
19 Cf. Lewis Mumford, *The Story of Utopias*, pp. 202ff.
20 Distinction made by Bertrand de Jouvenel, *L'art de la conjecture* (Monaco, Editions du Rocher, 1964), p. 13.
21 Quoted by William Barrett, op. cit., p. 142.
22 Martin G. Plattel, *Utopian and Critical Thinking* (Pittsburgh, Duquesne University Press, 1972), p. 83.
23 Cf. Theodore Adorno, 'Zur Logik der Sozialwissenschaften', *Kölner Zeitschrift für Soziologie*, vol. 14 (1962), p. 262.
24 Ulam, op. cit., p. 399.
25 Gerber, op. cit., p. 76.
26 Robert Nisbet, *Community and Power* (New York, Oxford University Press, 1962), p. xvii.

CHAPTER 3

1 Cf. Reinhard Bendix, *Nationbuilding and Citizenship* (Chichester, John Wiley & Sons, 1964).
2 Alexis de Tocqueville, *The Old Regime and the French Revolution* (New York, Doubleday, 1955), p. 176.
3 Quoted after Gunther Roth, *The Social Democrats in Imperial Germany* (Totowa, Bedminster Press, 1963), p. 52.

CHAPTER 4

1 Emile Durkheim, *Socialism and Saint Simon*, trans. Charlotte Sattler (London, Routledge & Kegan Paul, 1959), pp. 19–20.
2 Ludwig von Mises, *Die Gemeinwirtschaft*, 1922; English edition: *Socialism, an Economic and Sociological Analysis*, trans. J. Kahane (London, Jonathan Cape, 1936), p. 20.
3 Joseph A. Schumpeter, *Capitalism, Socialism, and Democracy* (London, George Allen & Unwin, 1943), p. 167.
4 Ibid., p. 143.
5 Henry Smith, *The Economics of Socialism Reconsidered* (London, Oxford University Press, 1962), p. 113.
6 Karl Korsch, *Marxism and Philosophy*, trans. Fred Halliday (London, New Left Books, 1970), p. 126.
7 Gustave Le Bon, *The Psychology of Socialism* (London, T. Fisher Unwin, 1899), p. 5.

CHAPTER 5

1 Gustave Le Bon, *The Psychology of Socialism* (London, T. Fisher Unwin, 1899), p. 84.
2 Werner Sombart, *Socialism and the Social Movement* (1896), trans. M. Epstein (London, Dent, 1909), p. 14.
3 Gunther Roth, *The Social Democrats in Imperial Germany* (Totowa, Bedminster Press, 1963), p. 124.

CHAPTER 6

1 Alex Inkeles, 'Models and Issues in the Analysis of Soviet Society', *Survey* N.60 (July 1966), pp. 3–14.
2 A. G. Meyer, 'Authority in Communist Political Systems', in Lewis J. Ediger (ed.), *Political Leadership in Industrialized Societies* (New York, John Wiley & Sons, 1967), p. 67.
3 William H. Friedland and Carl G. Rosberg Jr (eds), *African Socialism* (Stanford University Press, 1964), pp. 8–9.
4 Isaac Deutscher, *Marxism in Our Time*, ed. Tamara Deutscher (Berkeley, The Rampart Press, 1971), p. 201.
5 Z. Bauman, 'Officialdom and Class', *The Social Analysis of Class Structure*, ed. Frank Parkin (London, Tavistock, 1975).
6 Deutscher, op. cit., p. 23.
7 Maximilien Rubel, *Karl Marx, Essai de biographie intellectuelle* (Paris, Editions Marcel Rivière et Cie, 1971), p. xxi.

CHAPTER 7

1 Erich Fromm, *The Dogma of Christ and other Essays* (New York, Anchor Books, 1963), p. 20.

2 Antonio Gramsci, *The Modern Prince and other writings*, trans. L. Marks (London, Laurence & Wishort, 1957), p. 117.

3 Perry Anderson, 'Problems of Socialist Strategy', in *Towards Socialism*, ed. Perry Anderson and Robin Blackburn (Ithaca, Cornell University Press, 1966), p. 222.

4 George Lichtheim, 'The Future of Socialism', in *The Radical Papers*, ed. Irving Howe (New York, Anchor Books, 1966), pp. 65, 70.

5 Lewis Coser and Irving Howe, 'Images of Socialism', in ibid., p. 24.

6 Norman Birnbaum, 'Late Capitalism in the United States', in *The Revival of American Socialism, Selected Papers of the Socialist Scholars Conference*, ed. George Fischer (New York, Oxford University Press, 1971), p. 152.

7 Martin Nicolaus, 'The Crisis of Late Capitalism', in ibid., p. 12.

8 C. Wright Mills, *The Sociological Imagination* (New York, Oxford University Press, 1959), pp. 3, 11.

9 James O'Connor, 'Merging Thought with Feeling', in Fischer (ed.), *The Revival of American Socialism*, pp. 22ff.

10 Ibid., p. 14.

11 Harry S. Kariel, 'Expanding the Political Present', in *Seeing Beyond – Personal, Social, and Political Alternatives*, ed. Dennis Pirages (Reading, Addison-Wesley, 1971), pp. 283ff.

12 Herbert Marcuse, *Counter Revolution and Revolt* (Boston, Beacon Press, 1972), pp. 16–17.

13 Judith N. Sklar, *After Utopia, The Decline of Political Faith* (Princeton University Press, 1969), p. 267.

CHAPTER 8

1 Perry Anderson, 'Problems of Socialist Strategy', in *Towards Socialism*, ed. Perry Anderson and Robin Blackburn (Ithaca, Cornell University Press, 1966), pp. 231, 234.

2 C. B. Macpherson, Revolution and Ideology in the Late Twentieth Century', in *Nomos VIII* (New York, Atherton Press, 1967), p. 141.

3 Alexis de Tocqueville, *De la démocratie en Amérique* (Paris, 1854), vol. II, p. 151.

4 Max Horkheimer and Theodor W. Adorno, *Dialectic of Enlightenment*, trans. John Cumming (New York, Herder and Herder, 1972), p. 169. (London, Allen Lane, 1973.)

5 Max Horkheimer, *The Eclipse of Reason* (New York, 1947), p. 135.

6 Cf. Lelio Basso, 'What Kind of Individuality?', in *Essays on Socialist Humanism*, ed. Ken Coates (Nottingham, Spokesman Books, 1972), p. 57.

7 Stuart Hall, 'The Supply of Demand', in *Out of Apathy*, ed. E. P. Thompson (London, Steven & Sons, 1960), p. 73.

8 Paul A. Baran, *The Longer View*, ed. John O'Neill (New York, Monthly Review Press, 1969), pp. 25, 72.

9 T. B. Bottomore, 'The Class Structure in Western Europe', in *Contemporary Europe: Class, Status, and Power*, ed. Margaret Scotford

Archer and Salvador Giner (London, Weidenfeld and Nicolson, 1971), p. 406.

10 André Gorz, 'Work and Consumption', in *Towards Socialism*, ed. Perry Anderson and Robin Blackburn (Ithaca, Cornell University Press, 1966), pp. 316, 319, 335.

11 James O'Connor, 'Merging Thought with Feeling', in Fischer (ed.), *The Revival of American Socialism* (New York, Oxford University Press, 1971), pp. 29–30.

12 T. B. Bottomore, 'Industry, Work, and Socialism, in *Socialist Humanism*, ed. Erich Fromm (New York, Doubleday, 1966), pp. 401–2.

13 Svetozar Stojanović, *Between Ideals and Reality*, trans. Gerson S. Sher (New York, Oxford University Press, 1973), p. 121.

14 Roger Garaudy, *The Crisis in Communism, the turning point of socialism*, trans. Peter and Betty Ross (New York, Grove Press, 1970), pp. 144–5.

15 Svetozar Stojanović, op. cit., pp. 119, 130.

16 Ibid., p. 166.

17 Henri Lefebvre, *Everyday Life in the Modern World* (London, Allen Lane, 1971), p. 146.

18 Horkheimer and Adorno, op. cit., p. 16.

19 'Elements of Antisemitism: The Limits of Enlightenment', in ibid., pp. 170, 197.

20 Herbert Marcuse, *Counter Revolution and Revolt* (Boston, Beacon Press, 1972), p. 132.

21 Ibid., pp. 50, 51.

22 Karl E. Klare, 'The Critique of Everyday Life', in *The Unknown Dimension*, ed. Dick Howard and Karl E. Klare (New York, Basic Books, 1972), pp. 15–16.

23 Ibid., p. 24.

24 Isaac Deutscher, *Marxism in Our Time*, ed. Tamara Deutscher (Berkeley, The Rampart Press, 1971), p. 74.

25 Daniel Bell, *The Coming of Post-Industrial Society* (New York, Basic Books, 1973), p. 486. (London, Heinemann, 1974.)

26 Leszek Kołakowski, *Obecność Mitu* (Paris, Instytut Literacki, 1972), p. 85.

CHAPTER 9

1 Frank Parkin, *Class Inequality and Political Order* (St. Albans, Paladin, 1972, pp. 81ff.

2 Ibid., pp. 90–1.

3 Irving Howe, 'The Welfare State', in *The Revival of American Socialism, Selected Papers of the Socialist Scholars Conference*, ed. George Fischer (New York, Oxford University Press, 1971), p. 65.

4 J. H. Westergaard, 'The Withering Away of Class: A Contemporary Myth', in *Towards Socialism*, ed. Perry Anderson and Robin Blackburn (Ithaca, Cornell University Press, 1966), pp. 105ff.

5 *The Revival of American Socialism*, p. 8.

6 Perry Anderson, 'Problems of Socialist Strategy', in *Towards Socialism*, ed. Perry Anderson and Robin Blackburn (Ithaca, Cornell University Press, 1966), p. 241.

7 André Gorz, 'Work and Consumption', in *Towards Socialism*, op. cit., pp. 328, 329.

Index